At Women's Expense

At Women's Expense

STATE POWER AND THE
POLITICS OF FETAL RIGHTS

Cynthia R. Daniels

HARVARD UNIVERSITY PRESS
Cambridge, Massachusetts
London, England   1993

Copyright © 1993 by the President and Fellows of Harvard
    College

Printed in the United States of America
10   9   8   7   6   5   4   3   2   1

This book is printed on acid-free paper, and its binding
materials have been chosen for strength and durability.

Library of Congress Cataloging-in-Publication Data

Daniels, Cynthia R.
    At women's expense : state power and the politics of
fetal rights / Cynthia R. Daniels.
        p.   cm.
    Includes bibliographical references and index.
    ISBN 0-674-05043-6 (alk. paper)
    1. Fetus—Legal status, laws, etc.—United States.
2. Pregnant women—Legal status, laws, etc.—United
States. I. Title.
    KF481.D36   1993
    342.73'0878—dc20
    [347.302878]
                                        93-4102
                                            CIP

With love and gratitude, for Bob and Katie

Contents

Introduction:
Fetal Rights, Gender Difference,
and Political Power

A CESARIAN section is performed on a terminally ill woman against her will, resulting in the deaths of both mother and child. Women employees at a battery production plant are required to undergo surgical sterilization or prove they are infertile in order to keep their jobs. A woman who used drugs during pregnancy is convicted of delivering cocaine to a minor through the umbilical cord and sentenced to fifteen years' strict probation, including random drug tests and reproductive monitoring.

THE NOTION that the fetus has rights, as a patient and a citizen, separate from the pregnant woman's, has generated a deep crisis in reproductive relations in the United States. It is a crisis which throws into question women's rights to self-sovereignty, to work, and to due process under the law. It is a crisis which raises profound questions about the meaning of gender difference for women's relation to state power, and one that suggests the tenuous nature of women's hold on liberal citizenship.

Technological, social, political, and economic developments in the second half of the twentieth century have challenged the "organic unity" of the pregnant woman and the fetus. Scientific advances made it possible to separate the fertilized egg from the woman, and the fetus from the pregnant body, and to see and treat the fetus as a second patient. Court decisions granted the fetus limited legal rights in cases involving criminal negligence and inheritance. A powerful anti-abortion movement presented visual images of the fetus as a fully formed "preborn baby," a free-floating being temporarily housed in the womb, but with interests and needs of its own. In the broader public culture, the idea of "selfless motherhood" was undermined by women's claims to abortion rights and to equal employment outside the home.

These developments created not just a sense of social dislocation in men's and women's relation to reproduction, but a crisis in gender power relations. At stake in the new politics of fetal rights is not control over fetal health but the mediation and consolidation of the ultimate power that women have: the power to give birth.

At the heart of the politics of fetal rights is this question: Does the ability to carry a fetus to term necessarily change women's relationship to the state and alter women's standing as citizens in the liberal polity? As the fetus is animated and personified in public culture, the power of the state to regulate the behavior of women—both pregnant and potentially pregnant—is strengthened. Women's rights as citizens are potentially made contingent by fetal rights. They can be revoked or qualified by the state's higher interest in the fetus.

A new kind of reproductive politics has emerged on the American political stage. In the past the focus was on either reproductive choice (the beginning of pregnancy) or the politics of motherhood (the aftermath of pregnancy). In the politics of reproductive choice, women sought control over how and when they became pregnant, over sterilization, and over the decision to continue or end a pregnancy. In the politics of motherhood, women sought to define for themselves the contours of good and proper mothering. The new politics of fetal rights focuses on the politics of pregnancy itself—on mediating and regulating what some now characterize as the *social relationship* between the pregnant woman and the fetus.

By 1992, criminal charges had been brought against 167 pregnant women for delivering drugs to the fetus through the umbilical cord, for prenatal child neglect or abuse (by consuming alcohol or drugs during pregnancy), or for manslaughter, in cases where a pregnancy ended in the delivery of a stillborn baby.[1] Hospital authorities in twenty-four states have sought court orders to force pregnant women to undergo medical procedures such as cesarian sections, maternal blood transfusions, or fetal surgery or transfusions. In all but three cases, those court orders were granted, and in two states court orders were granted for the hospital detention of pregnant women.[2] During the 1980s, hundreds of companies instituted fetal protection policies in the workplace, which excluded women entirely from certain forms of work unless they could prove that they had been surgically sterilized or were infertile, or which required women to make regular reports of their "fertility status" to their employers.[3]

Although physicians and social workers have attempted in the past to impose what they consider to be proper behavior on women during pregnancy, never before have attempts been made to encode such imperatives in law or to prosecute women who deviated from them. Fueled by an ideology of fetal rights, the state could now seize the pregnant woman's body as public property, restricting her access to work, jailing her for drinking or for failing to follow doctor's orders, or forcing her to undergo major surgery against her will.

The fetus has emerged as the newest "social actor" in the American conservative imagination. Portrayed by the fetal rights movement as the tiniest citizen, the fetus is depicted as an independent being with needs, interests, and rights separate from and often opposed to the pregnant woman's. Attempts to "protect" the fetus against the actions of the pregnant woman did not arise until the legalization of abortion and the development of an anti-abortion movement. The anti-abortion movement cast the fetus as a fully formed baby from the earliest stages of pregnancy and cast abortion as a form of murder. A new social mythology encouraged the view that some women were not just bad mothers but "anti-mothers," who violated their most fundamental natural instincts and who threatened to destroy the institution of motherhood altogether. Fetal rights advocates argued that, once a woman chose to continue a pregnancy, she gained a "duty to care" for the fetus in utero—to insure that the fetus was born with "sound mind and body."[4] The broader public discourse on motherhood bred a deep suspicion of women who, if they did not terminate fetal life, might still damage or harm fetal health through their selfish or negligent behavior while pregnant. Women could no longer be trusted to subordinate their self-interest to the interests of the fetus.

Those opposed to the concept of fetal rights have challenged this characterization as yet another attempt to reinstate social domination over women. Feminists argue that fetal rights cases represent an effort to reassert masculine control of the female body through the power of the state. Opponents of fetal rights argue that such cases seek to reestablish the boundaries within which women reproduce and to encode these boundaries in law—to regulate and control not just reproductive choice, but the internal relationship between the pregnant woman and the fetus. The intensity of debates over fetal rights suggests the depth of the current crisis in gender power relations and in men's and women's reproductive roles.

At the beginning of the twentieth century, the U.S. Supreme Court expressed the essence of the state's interest in motherhood in its decision in Muller v. Oregon: "As healthy mothers are essential to vigorous offspring, the physical well-being of women becomes an object of public interest and care in order to preserve the strength and vigor of the race."[5] The state's interest in women as a "national resource" in this sense justified a wide range of restrictions on women's rights, restrictions which have for the most part been struck down by anti-discrimination law. Now, at the end of the twentieth century, state protectionism has been fundamentally transformed by the state's new interest in fetal health: the rhetoric of protectionism has fundamentally shifted from maternal to fetal health.

Current fetal rights cases suggest that women's fundamental rights to self-determination may be jeopardized in new ways by the state's interest in the fetus. This interest could potentially be invoked not just from the moment of fetal viability, or even from the moment of conception, but from the moment a woman becomes fertile. One fetal rights advocate has suggested that the state might even have an obligation to protect the "pre-conceived."[6] The politics of fetal rights thus implicates the rights of all women as a class, as the relationship of each woman to the state is determined by her potential to give birth.

Many attempts to criminalize, restrict, or regulate the behavior of fertile women have been successfully challenged in the courts. But these very attempts tell us something important about the ways in which women's association with reproduction continues to be used as the basis for efforts to undermine women's status as citizens. Fetal rights cases raise fundamental questions about the difference between men's and women's relationship to citizenship and state power. In understanding the political significance of gender difference, it's useful to consider three related dimensions of political power, each of which is best illustrated by one of the fetal rights cases examined in this book.

The first dimension is the power of *self-sovereignty*. The forced medical treatment of pregnant women, represented by the Angela Carder case presented in Chapter 2, illustrates the unique set of issues raised by pregnancy for women's right to bodily integrity. The right to self-sovereignty, defined here as the simple right to bodily integrity, is the primary foundation of liberal citizenship. More fundamental than the right to vote and to be recognized as a formal citizen, more fundamental than the right to work and to earn one's living, is the right to control one's body. There are at least two conditions under which a liberal polity may deny a citizen's most fundamental rights: when a person lacks the capacity for self-governance, or when the exercise of one person's right to self-sovereignty threatens the health or well-being of another.[7] The question raised by fetal rights cases is whether the condition of pregnancy (or potential pregnancy) constitutes a legitimate basis for limiting women's right to self-sovereignty on both of these grounds.

Fetal rights cases involving women's right to bodily integrity also suggest the inadequacies of the classical liberal concepts of individualism, privacy, and self-determination to defend women's rights in pregnancy. Such concepts seem both essential to women's empowerment and yet incapable of capturing the potential, developmental, and relational nature of pregnancy or the deeply social nature of reproduction. The politics of fetal rights thus suggests the need to rethink the concept of self-sovereignty from the point of view of the female body.

The second dimension of political power is the power of *political agency*—the ability to transform public structures (in work and politics) to reflect one's needs, interests, and concerns. The Johnson Controls case analyzed in Chapter 3, involving the attempt of one company to exclude women from work based on their fertility, most clearly illustrates this aspect of power.

For women, gaining the power of political agency has meant acquiring the ability to articulate women's reproductive and familial concerns within the public spheres of politics and work.

Paradoxically, this process of "going public" has both empowered women and drawn them into more subtle and complex mechanisms of social control.[8] The articulation of women's reproductive needs in the public sphere has also reinforced assumptions about immutable differences between the sexes. State policies which address gender difference might simply encode a gender ethos which reinforces traditional maternalism and institutionalizes the differential standing of men and women in politics and work.[9] But the denial of difference seems equally problematic, as it reinforces standards of public life which seem masculine at their heart. Fetal rights cases suggest that public structures of power must be "degendered" from the social, historical, and biological standpoint of women.

The third dimension of political power is the power of *moral discourse*—the ability to legitimate the shared moral norms and cultural beliefs which undergird power relations. The Jennifer Johnson case discussed in Chapter 4, involving the criminal prosecution of a drug-addicted pregnant woman, most clearly illustrates this aspect of political power. One of the most central powers of the state is its function as a social and moral regulator which defines acceptable and unacceptable forms of behavior.[10] The moral authority of the state becomes most potent in times of real or perceived social crisis.

When there is no consensus in popular discourse on a particular social problem, the state has great power to shape public perceptions of volatile social issues. Legal cases, like the Jennifer Johnson case, take on great symbolic meaning as they crystallize questions during periods of social, political, or economic transformation. The state's response to such "signal" events can be pivotal in determining where we assign culpability or blame for a problem and how we define appropriate solutions.

Political debates are partly social dramas, in which social actors compete for the power to shape public discourse and to legitimate and institutionalize their worldview through the formal mechanisms of government power.[11] Those who seek the prosecution of pregnant women for drug or alcohol abuse present visions of "anti-mothers" whose behavior violates the most fundamental instincts of motherhood. Those who oppose prosecution offer counter-images of a "reproductive 1984" in which state agents, employers, physicians, therapists, and even bartenders become moral enforcers of patriarchal motherhood. The decision of the state to affirm one narrative over the other holds implications far beyond the particular legal questions, as it affirms a broader worldview of gender roles and power relations.

The very attempt to prosecute pregnant women for addiction has created a powerful social mythology about women. The power of this mythology may at times eclipse the power of law. Although women's rights may ultimately be upheld in the courts, a broader public culture may continue to endorse resentment toward women and more subtle forms of social coercion against those who transgress the boundaries of traditional motherhood. Social anxiety and resentment are most easily projected onto those women who are perceived as most distant from white, middle-class norms. Political power may ultimately rest not on the technical precedent of legal rights, but on the symbols, images, and narratives used to represent women in this larger public culture.

1

Fetal Animation:
The Political and Cultural
Emergence of Fetal Rights

DURING the 1980s a number of cultural, political, legal, and technological developments converged to bring the fetus into public consciousness as an independent and autonomous being. In law and in popular culture, the fetus was treated as physically separate from the pregnant woman and was personified—granted interests, concerns, and needs which may conflict with the pregnant woman's. The fetus came to be seen as a tiny "person" housed within the pregnant woman's body, a vulnerable child-citizen with rights and interests to be protected by the state.

While the characterization of the fetus as a fully formed person was not new, technological and legal changes during the 1980s contributed to unprecedented attempts to mediate and control the internal "relationship" between the pregnant woman and the fetus.[1] As the fetus grew larger in pregnancy, so too grew the public interest in the woman.

The public coercion of pregnant women fueled by fetal rights cases throughout the 1980s was completely without precedent in American society. What contributed to so dramatic a shift in the law? What spurred this virtual revolution in popular culture? During the 1970s and 1980s, a legal ideology emerged that endowed the fetus with independent rights from its "host" mother. New medical technologies allowed the public to see the fetus in utero through ultrasound and intrauterine photography. These technologies, which allowed women to have greater control over their pregnancies, made it possible for others to control pregnancy as well. Capitalizing on such developments, a powerful anti-abortion movement waged a major media war by presenting the visual image of the fetus as a fully formed "preborn baby."

The politics of fetal rights that emerged was generated by forces which empowered women as well as by forces which sought to institutionalize new forms of masculine control over the female body. Feminists argued that motherhood was no longer essential to womanhood—that procreation, like heterosexuality and monogamy, was voluntary. Theorists such as Simone de Beauvoir and Shulamith Firestone cast pregnancy as a form of biological servitude supporting masculine domination.[2] Although the idea of voluntary motherhood was essential to gender equality, it also generated its own transformations in the nature of dominative power. Seen as a social institution, and not a biological necessity, motherhood became susceptible to new regulatory forces, as judges, physicians, and state administrators sought to mediate and control the most intimate details of pregnancy and reproduction.

There are two senses in which we can speak of "fetal animation." Historically, pregnancy was not recognized until quickening—when the fetus was literally animated with life. For instance, in nineteenth century America, as in many other cultures around the world, abortion was not restricted until after quickening.[3] But in the contemporary context, fetal animation also refers to the public visualization of the fetus in public discourse, through film and popular literature. As the visualization of fetal life moved deeper into pregnancy, depicting fetal development at earlier stages, so too grew the social impulse to mediate and regulate the behavior of pregnant women. By the 1980s, this impulse—fast becoming an imperative—was reflected in science, in popular culture, and in law.

The Fetus and the Law

Not long ago the idea that maternal interests and fetal interests could be legally opposed did not exist in American law. Having no separate legal status under common law, the fetus did not gain rights as an individual until it existed outside of the mother's body. Any recognition of fetal interests was construed purely as an extension of the interests of the mother.

The earliest fetal rights case was Dietrich v. Northampton, brought in 1884 by a woman in Northampton, Massachusetts, who fell as a result of a defect in the town highway and subsequently miscarried a four-to-five-month-old fetus. She sued the town for damages in tort court. Writing for the court, Oliver Wendell Holmes argued that the unborn fetus had been lost "before he became a person." The case, he argued, concerned "whether an infant dying before it was able to live separated from its mother could be said to have become a person recognized by the law as capable of having a *locus standi* in courts." Legal action, he argued, was dependent upon the child having achieved "some degree of quasi independent life." Holmes denied an award to the woman on the basis that the fetus was "a part of the mother at the time of the injury."[4]

For fifty years following the *Dietrich* decision, the law recognized only limited rights of the fetus, and granted such rights only after the fetus had been born alive. As one justice put it, the unborn child "is not regarded as a person until it sees the light of day."[5] The earliest deviation from this legal standard came in the form of inheritance cases, which recognized for limited legal reasons the existence of the fetus before birth. A fetus could inherit property upon its birth even though the fetus did not technically exist as a person at the time of death of its benefactor.[6]

While the courts provided such limited inheritance rights for a fetus throughout the early twentieth century, the precedent set by *Dietrich* generally viewed the fetus as a part of the woman's body and not a separate person having rights and interests of its own. Such a view had its limitations. For instance, it provided no means by which parents could recover damages for injuries inflicted on a fetus before birth, even after the live birth of the child. The *Dietrich* decision itself failed to compensate the pregnant woman for her loss.

In 1946, the case of Bonbrest v. Kotz allowed a father to recover for fetal harm caused by a doctor during delivery, establishing the existence of limited rights for the fetus before birth.[7] The case broke precedent with *Dietrich*, but still maintained that the fetus gained no separate recognition until it passed the point of viability, very late in pregnancy. In addition, such rights were conferred upon the fetus only after it was born alive. Other cases established the rights of parents to compensation for prenatal injuries in cases involving physical assault on the pregnant woman or injuries from automobile accidents.

In 1960, the *Dietrich* precedent was further eroded by a pivotal case that allowed parents to recover for injuries inflicted on the fetus before the point of viability. The case of Brennan v. Smith granted recovery for a fetus harmed in an automobile accident. Whereas prenatal injuries experienced in the moments just before birth had already been established in law, the *Brennan* case clearly affirmed the rights of a fetus before it was capable of living outside the mother's womb: "the viability distinction has no relevance to the injustice of denying recovery for harm which can be proved to have resulted from the wrongful act of another. Whether viable or not at the time of the injury, the child sustains the same harm after birth."[8]

As technological advances made it possible to prove a causal link between injuries sustained in early fetal development and medical problems experienced by the child after birth, the impetus to hold liable those responsible for such injuries became more and more compelling. Why should women not be able to sue in cases where physicians, employers, or corporations harmed the developing fetus, either directly or through negligence? In fact, some analysts now suggest that the right to recovery exists for the "preconceived" as well—that parents may sue for damages in cases where birth defects are caused by parental exposure to mutagenic substances, such as Agent Orange, not only before birth, but before conception.[9]

Another major contribution of the *Brennan* case was the court's statement that "the child has a legal right to begin life with a sound mind and body."[10] This affirmed not only the right of the child to sue for damages, but also the right of the child to be protected from negligence or harm in utero. This precedent had far-ranging consequences which would emerge in the 1980s.

The spirit of legal decisions in the late 1970s, while endowing the fetus with rights independent of the mother, viewed injuries to the fetus as synonymous with injuries to the mother (or father). Court cases such as *Brennan* were motivated by a desire to give parents the power to recover for prenatal harm. The precedent set by *Brennan* and affirmed many times over throughout the 1970s provided pregnant women with a powerful legal tool for recovering damages from third parties (including abusive husbands) who, through criminal or negligent behavior, threatened the health of their wanted child. The right of the child (and its parents) to sue for compensation for prenatal injuries is now recognized by law in almost every state, but this right is still generally contingent upon the live birth of the child—after the child becomes a "person" at birth. Such legal precedents, while recognizing the additional interests of the pregnant woman, do not affirm the separate legal personhood of the fetus.

As long as fetal rights remained contingent upon live birth, and as long as the spirit of the law remained focused on the injustice done to the mother as well as to the fetus, the establishment of fetal rights posed no threat to pregnant women's autonomy. As Dawn Johnsen argues, such cases "did not conceive of the fetus as separate from the woman, but took legal cognizance of the fact that the woman was pregnant."[11] The law assumed the fetus was an inseparable part of the pregnant woman's body and sought simply to compensate the child and parents for negligent or criminal behavior.

Conservative advocates seized on the legal opportunity to expand the grounds for fetal rights. In promoting the idea of fetal rights, Jeffrey Parness recounts many legal injustices suffered by pregnant women. In these stories women lose wanted pregnancies due to the recklessness of drunken drivers, the violence of muggers or rapists, careless mistreatment by doctors, or the willful negligence of corporations who poison women with toxins or place them in unsafe workplaces.

"Because states bestow upon the fetus and other unborn virtually no criminal law protection from intentional infliction of nonfatal injury by a third party, great injustices may prevail. The assailant who repeatedly strikes an expectant woman, intending to damage and actually damaging the fetus, can often be prosecuted only for crimes against the woman. Assault on the fetus does not constitute a separate crime." As a result, Parness argues, "The interests in protecting potential life are not fully vindicated."[12]

Parness promotes the establishment of fetal rights before birth by presenting cases where pregnant women miscarried after severe beatings by their husbands. Because of the "live birth" rule, these women had no way to recover damages for the loss of their pregnancy. In these cases, he points to the inadequacy of the law:

"Thus, Smith from the California case of *People v. Smith* apparently could not have been prosecuted for criminal abortion had he acted in Illinois, because he only beat his pregnant wife with his fists for an hour, kicked her in the stomach, shouted that he did not want her fetus to survive, and said, 'Bleed, baby, bleed.'"[13] Similarly, in the cases of Hollis v. Commonwealth (in Kentucky) and in Keeler v. Superior Court (in California), Parness argues, men who caused the intentional loss of their "unborn children" by severely beating their wives late in pregnancy could be prosecuted only for assault on the woman and not for the death of the fetus.

There were clearly problems with the law as it stood, both for pregnant women themselves and for those who would later affirm the rights of the fetus against the rights of women. While the law could compensate parents for prenatal injuries, ironically it could not compensate them for prenatal death. Injuries sustained in utero were legally recognized if they were severe enough to cause permanent injury to the fetus after birth, but not if they were severe enough to cause death. Because the fetus became a legal person only at birth, there was no cause of action for fetal loss or death.

As modern technology made it possible to preserve the lives of fetuses that would not normally be viable, conservative advocates argued that the "born alive" rule was outmoded.[14] Why, Parness asks, should the destruction of fetal life one moment before birth be so different from the murder of an infant moments after? As he argues, the legal system "too often treats differently the actor whose culpable conduct terminates the existence of a nine month old fetus and the actor who causes the death of an infant which had existed independently of the mother for an instant."[15]

For Parness, the answer to such injustice is to close the gap between the born and the unborn. "Feticide" laws, such as an Iowa statute which prosecutes for murder anyone who "intentionally terminates a human pregnancy after the end of the second trimester of pregnancy," could help to protect not only women's rights to compensation, but also the legal integrity of "preborn life."[16]

A dramatic shift in opinion began to emerge in the courts during the 1980s as a result of pressures brought by such advocates.

Exactly one hundred years after the Massachusetts courts set precedent in the *Dietrich* case by denying the independent rights of the fetus, Massachusetts again set precedent in the opposite direction by affirming for the first time the personhood of the fetus before birth. In 1984, Commonwealth v. Cass recognized as a "person" a fetus that died as a result of injuries caused by an automobile accident.[17] Since then, at least ten states have enacted laws which allow the prosecution for homicide of those who "murder" a fetus.[18]

Since 1984 there has been a dramatic rise in the number of cases involving prosecution for fetal homicide. Nearly every newspaper story detailing the murder of a pregnant woman now addresses at least the possibility of prosecution for the homicide of the fetus as well. Dozens of states have enacted feticide laws, giving the fetus full legal status as a person under criminal and tort law.[19]

While discarding the live birth rule, most states still do not grant rights to a fetus until it has reached the point of viability. That is, one can be prosecuted for the murder of a fetus only once it has reached the point where it could have, in theory, existed separately from the woman. As long as those charged with endangering the health of pregnant women remained third parties— from abusive husbands and incompetent doctors to negligent employers and violent criminals—the provision of rights to the fetus increased the rights and powers of women. As Dawn Johnsen, legal counsel for the National Abortion Rights Action League, argues, "Holding third parties responsible for the negligent or criminal destruction of fetuses is therefore consistent with, and even enhances, the protection of pregnant women's interests."[20] But soon to emerge on the legal and political scene was a movement to cast women themselves as the "criminal actors" who posed the gravest threat to fetal health, through their ignorance, their negligence, or their own criminal behavior. As the language of the law shifted attention from the loss experienced by the parent or parents to the loss "experienced" by the fetus, it began to create the legal fiction of the fetus's existence separate from the woman's body.[21] This transformation in the law was set within the context of a larger cultural and scientific discourse which endowed the fetus with independent life.

The Scientific and Cultural Construction of Fetal Rights

The construction of fetal rights was deeply related to the development of scientific and cultural images of the fetus. Among the technological advances contributing to the image of the fetus as an independent and autonomous being were ultrasound and intrauterine photography, fetal surgery, and medical treatments for premature infants. Each of these made the fetus more visible, and made less significant the perceived difference between the "unborn" and the "born" child.

The idea that the fetus was separable from the woman was based not only on attempts to wrest reproductive control from women, but also in technological inventions which made it possible for the fetus to exist outside of the woman's body. As Emily Martin observes, "Human eggs, sperm, and embryos can now be moved from body to body or out of and back into the same female body. The organic unity of the fetus and mother can no longer be assumed, and all these newly fragmented parts can now be subjected to market forces, ordered, produced, bought and sold."[22]

Ultrasound technology, developed during the 1960s and now widely used during pregnancy, provided the visual imagery of the fetus as a "tiny baby" housed inside the pregnant woman's body. With the help of technicians and physicians, potential parents came to "see" the fetal image as the image of a newly formed baby. Ultrasound imagery was distinct enough to suggest the similarities between the fetus and the baby (through the shadowy images of head, limbs, even fingers and toes), while it was vague enough to mask the dramatic differences between the fetus and the newborn infant (such as the immature brain, central nervous system, and lungs).

The fetal imagery produced by ultrasound technology allowed the creation of a great imaginary drama of fetal development—a drama pursued as much by expectant parents as by health practitioners eager to display their latest wizardry. Ultrasound images treated as "baby's first picture" joined dramatic intrauterine photography to produce images of the fetus as a separate living being at earlier and earlier stages of development.[23]

In order to publicly display the fetus in photographic and video images, the pregnant woman had to become transparent. The development of fetal imagery led to a fundamental transformation in how we think about the pregnant woman's body. With the aid of visual technologies, fetal development became an event for public viewing. As Rosalind Petchesky has observed, fetal technologies have disrupted "the very definition, as traditionally understood, of 'inside' and 'outside' a woman's body, of pregnancy as an 'interior' experience."[24] Once this very private, internal process became publicly visible the possibility arose for the public control of pregnancy.

Neonatal Technology and the Question of Viability

The fiction of the fetus's independence from the woman's body was further enhanced by technological advances which made it possible to save premature infants. The changing criteria of fetal viability fueled fantasies about the ability of the fetus to survive outside the woman's body from the first moments following conception.

In Roe v. Wade, the Supreme Court established that the state's interest in the fetus becomes compelling at viability, that is, when the fetus is "potentially able to live outside the mother's womb, albeit with artificial aid."[25] Once the fetus has the potential for "meaningful" (and not just "momentary") life outside of the mother's womb, the state has an overriding interest in preserving that life, even if it conflicts with the woman's right to privacy.

Women's right to abortion has thus been contingent upon the shifting definition of fetal viability. Roe originally defined the age of viability as twenty-eight weeks of pregnancy, but recognized that it may be as early as twenty-four weeks. Rather than setting a strict time limit on abortions or establishing an arbitrary measure of viability, like fetal birth weight, it left the question of viability up to the woman's physician. Currently, fewer than 1 percent of all abortions are performed after twenty weeks of gestation and only 10 percent are performed between the thirteenth and nineteenth weeks.[26]

How is viability defined? Is a fetus viable if it has a 10 percent chance of survival? If it survives for a few days, weeks, or months but has no chance of long-term survival? If it survives with severe handicaps that will ensure a life of pain and suffering? Before delivery viability is purely hypothetical. How then do we measure the viability of a fetus?

Mary Ellen Avery, a professor of pediatrics at Harvard Medical School who has conducted a national study of premature infants, reports that about half of all babies born after twenty-four weeks survive and about one-tenth of those born between twenty-three and twenty-four weeks survive, but "the odds of survival become infinitesimal before twenty-three weeks."[27] Cultural images have encouraged the perception that the fetus can survive at a much earlier age. Ronald Reagan once stated that premature infants had been born alive "even down to the *three month* stage and have lived to . . . grow up and be normal human beings."[28] Supreme Court Justice Sandra Day O'Connor suggested in a dissenting opinion in one abortion rights case that "fetal viability in the first trimester of pregnancy may be possible in the not too distant future."[29]

Despite these optimistic notions, the primary determinant of fetal survival is lung capacity, which typically develops at twenty-three to twenty-four weeks. Technological advances have so far been unable to pass the biological "line" set by lung development. Those who envision fetal survival before twenty-three weeks rely on the hope that technological intervention at earlier stages could take the form of an "artificial womb," a development currently thought to be scientifically (and financially) unrealistic.

The cultural expectation that fetuses will be able to survive at earlier and earlier stages of development has encouraged the perception of the fetus as an independent "person" from the earliest stages of pregnancy. Images in the media of two-pound "miracle" babies encourage the belief that the first- and second-trimester fetus is a smaller but physically complete version of the newborn infant. Anti-abortion activists such as Bernard Nathanson have encouraged this view: "Significant advances in science and technology in the past four years, such as realtime ultrasound scanning, fetal medicine, intra-uterine surgery, and in vitro fertilization have all confirmed beyond a reasonable doubt that prenatality is just another passage in our lives." Nathanson argues that abortion advocates have simply not come to grips with advances in modern technology, as they "cling to their flat earth credo."[30] Fetal personhood here is presented not as a moral, religious, or philosophical question, but as a technical and medical one. Science has simply "revealed" the humanness of the fetus.

Fetal Surgery and the Fetus as Second Patient

The idea of the fetus's independence has also been generated by the development of technologies for fetal surgery. With the advent of the fetoscope, a fine optical instrument that can be inserted into the woman's uterus through the abdominal wall, physicians can observe the fetus directly throughout most of a pregnancy and can diagnose and treat fetal diseases in utero.[31]

The speed with which new technologies changed the medical view of pregnancy was quite remarkable. Ultrasound imagery, which first made fetal diagnosis and treatment possible, only came into widespread use in the mid-1970s. By the mid-1980s, the testing and treatment of the fetus as a patient had become an accepted part of prenatal medicine. Ultrasound allowed physicians a window on the fetus and this visualization made a whole range of fetal therapies possible. Physicians could draw fetal blood samples and diagnose and treat conditions like acute anemia. Such technologies could empower women to save wanted pregnancies in cases where severe fetal abnormalities could be treated—or to decide to end pregnancies where they couldn't.

Prenatal surgery allowed physicians to treat the fetus directly without separating it from the woman's body. Surgery could now be performed by temporarily removing the fetus from the uterus (with the umbilical cord still attached), operating directly on it, and then replacing the fetus inside the womb.[32]

Each of these technological developments was seized upon by the media as medical marvel as well as by anti-abortion advocates in their own campaign to promote the fetus as a person. Fetal technologies merged with a powerful anti-abortion movement to create the public spectacle of fetal personhood. While fetal technologies could not themselves endow the fetus with independent life, they could suggest the ways in which such imagery could be used to shift the power of procreation and pregnancy away from women and toward the social institutions of science and the state.

Anti-Abortion Rhetoric and Imagery

Visual imagery presented by the anti-abortion movement reinforced the identification of the fetus as a baby. The development of fetal technologies, such as the fetoscope, provided powerful visual images for the anti-abortion movement to use. In Bernard Nathanson's words, new fetal technologies allowed the physician to come "eyeball to eyeball"[33] with the unborn baby: "one can see the six week old infant clearly. We can even study the face, fingers, toes—in fact, the entire young child."[34] Photographs used in anti-abortion campaigns focused on the fetal body parts that most resembled those of the newborn infant—the tiny feet of a ten-week-old fetus, the thumb approaching the mouth of the four-month-old "unborn child." The image of the tiny feet at ten weeks was used repeatedly in literature, on billboards and buttons, and in television campaigns to suggest the "humanness" of the fetus from the earliest moments of conception. "This is what your feet looked like when you were only ten weeks old" reads the caption from one anti-abortion pamphlet. "Perfectly formed? Yes! You even had fingerprints then."[35]

Such images sought to *personify* the fetus, to establish visual metaphors and encourage a complete identification between "pre-born life" and the newborn baby or even the full-grown human being. Through such imagery, the anti-abortion movement sought to promote the animation of the fetus as a person. It was a strategy that was as successful as it was dramatic. As Celeste Condit suggests in her fascinating study of the discourse of the abortion debate, "Personification here worked most effectively. The fetus was not only a person; it was *you*."[36] The image of the tiny feet operated as a synecdoche, a rhetorical device in which a part (the feet) represents the whole (the fetus). This tactic prevented any suggestion that the fetus was unformed, dependent, or lodged within the pregnant woman's body. As Condit observes, an "accurate, full picture of a young fetus includes features not associated with adult human beings—the placenta and the umbilical cord and, in a six-week fetus, even a 'tail.' With these and its ungainly face and head, off-balance and poorly formed, a young fetus looks like a wretched creature, bloody and undernourished."[37] In fact, at eight weeks most features of the fetus are so ill defined that it would be difficult for an uninformed observer to recognize it, viewed in its entirety, as distinctly human.

The anti-abortion movement focuses on the uterus rather than the woman. The uterus is not a part of the woman, but is the fetus's "sanctuary." The woman is not pregnant, but is an "expectant mother," a mother whose child has already been "born" at conception but not yet been released from the womb. As in the famous anti-abortion film *The Silent Scream*, the woman becomes the "maternal environment" which either nurtures and feeds the "preborn child" or threatens the child with "imminent extinction and death."[38]

The animation of fetal life through such imagery did more than just personify the fetus. As the fetus emerged as a person, the pregnant woman began literally to disappear from view. In much of the promotional literature of the anti-abortion movement, the fetus is visually severed from the mother, presented as an autonomous free-floating being, attached tenuously to the "mother ship" by the umbilical cord. Bernard Nathanson describes the fetus as a "person floating freely in a fluid environment . . . as free of gravity as any astronaut in space orbit." When the amniotic sac is broken in labor, "he feels the pull of gravity for the first time, like an astronaut re-entering the earth's relentless embrace."[39] But as the feminist scholar Barbara Katz Rothman has suggested, in this metaphor the pregnant woman becomes "empty space."[40] The invisible woman would reemerge later as a threat to the fetus's health, as a barrier to fetal life, as an actor alien to the fetus's interests.

Nathanson casts the conflict between the woman and the fetus at the most fundamental microbiologic level by arguing that the woman's body resists the very implantation of the egg from the first moment of fertilization, recognizing the conceptus as not of itself:

> when a pregnancy implants itself into the wall of the uterus at the eighth day following conception the defense mechanisms of the body . . . sense that this creature now settling down for a lengthy stay is an intruder, an alien, and must be expelled. Therefore an intense immunological attack is mounted on the pregnancy by the white blood cell elements, and through an ingenious and extraordinarily efficient defense system the unborn child succeeds in repelling the attack. In ten per cent or so of cases the defensive system fails and the pregnancy is lost as a spontaneous abortion or miscarriage. *Think how fundamental a lesson there is for us here: Even on the most minute microscopic scale the body has trained itself, or somehow in some inchoate way knows, how to recognize self from non-self.*[41]

The lesson here is also highly political: At even the most fundamental microscopic level, Nathanson suggests, there is a battle between the woman and the fetus from the earliest moments of life. By implication, the continuation of fetal life requires that it force itself against the social and biological impulses of the woman to expel, neglect, or otherwise threaten the life not only of the fetus, but even of the fertilized egg.

Instead of assuming the biological and emotional unity of mother and child, anti-abortionists depict a deeply fundamental conflict between them that must be mediated and regulated by outside forces for the fetus to survive. Once the biological unity between woman and fetus was broken, men could begin to control pregnancy itself. The regulation of that maternal-fetal relationship could begin not just once the point of viability had been passed, but from the moment of conception.

Although maternal-fetal conflicts were most explicit in anti-abortion literature, the notion of such conflicts also contributed to a broader public culture which challenged the status of pregnancy as the exclusive, private domain of women and legitimated in new ways male control over reproduction. When pregnancy became a public event, the power of men to control their progeny in utero was enhanced. Modern images of the fetus as autonomous from the woman coincided with ancient assumptions that the fetus was a "male seed" implanted into the womb. Aristotelian philosophy endowed the sperm with the power of life, as the agent which "ensouled" the fetus. The pregnant woman provided only the place for conception; the man provided the potent seed.[42] Cast in these terms, the power of procreation belongs to the fertile man.

Current debates over fetal rights again reflect the view that the fetus belongs to someone other than the pregnant woman, who simply acts as the "host" for the man's unborn child. Politicized characterizations of the biological processes of reproduction, in ancient times and today, have informed our understanding of the maternal-fetal relationship. The science of reproduction reflects assumptions about male power, rights, and ownership of the fetus as well as of the pregnant woman's body.

The marriage of anti-abortion ideology with the development of fetal technologies led to a powerful cultural movement which gave the fetus meaning and life outside of the woman's body. The fetus, temporarily "cradled" in the mother's womb, would become yet another source of male power and control over women's bodies. By the early 1980s, this concept of the independent fetus was clearly reflected in science, in popular culture, and in law.

The State's Interest in "Potential Life"

The technological possibility of early fetal separation from the pregnant woman has suggested that the state has an interest in fetal development from the earliest stages of life. Fetal rights advocates argue that the Supreme Court's decision in Roe v. Wade sanctioned and legitimated the state's interest in the fetus not only in the third trimester, but throughout pregnancy. In *Roe,* the Supreme Court recognizes and approves the state's "important and legitimate interest in protecting the potentiality of human life."[43] While affirming the woman's right to abortion in the first trimester and the joint interests of the woman and state in the second, *Roe* also explicitly affirms the dominance of the state's interest in the third trimester, once the fetus has passed the point of viability.

Although *Roe* prohibited the state from banning abortions before viability, fetal rights advocates argued that it implied the state's interest in potential life from the moment of conception. One legal advocate for fetal rights, Sam Balisy, proposes that "since even the fundamental right to an abortion may be denied under certain circumstances, the state should certainly have the power to restrict lesser supposed 'rights' to alcohol, tobacco and drugs when the use of such substances presents a serious risk of injury to the fetus."[44] Balisy contrasts the state's interest in the preservation of fetal health with the "pregnant mother's right to use alcohol, tobacco and drugs for physical and psychic pleasure," a contest in which surely the state's interest must prevail.[45]

With the Supreme Court's decision in Webster v. Reproductive Health Services, the court's emphasis on viability began to shift. *Webster* upheld a Missouri provision granting the fetus "all the rights, privileges, and immunities available to other persons, citizens, and residents of the state," and while it did not explicitly challenge the viability line in *Roe,* it made it increasingly possible for the construal of independent legal rights for the fetus before viability. The *Webster* decision, therefore, held important implications not only for women's rights to abortion but also for a whole range of state policies which sought to protect the fetus from "abuse" from the earliest moments of pregnancy.

In a critical legal shift, the 1992 Supreme Court decision in Planned Parenthood v. Casey affirmed the state's interest in fetal health from the moment of conception, even as the decision struck down state restrictions which placed an undue burden on women's right to abortion before viability. As Justice Sandra Day O'Connor, author of the court's opinion, stated, "It is a constitutional liberty of the woman to have some freedom to terminate her pregnancy. . . . The woman's liberty is not so unlimited, however, that from the outset the State cannot show its concern for the life of the unborn, and at a later point in fetal development the state's interest in life has sufficient force so that the right of the woman to terminate the pregnancy can be restricted."[46] While the state could not ban abortions before viability, it could actively discourage them by placing conditions upon women's choices—such as parental consent requirements for teen-aged women, or waiting periods for all women, or requirements that women receive information about adoption before having an abortion.

O'Connor argued explicitly that *Roe* recognized the right of the state to intervene in pregnancy even before viability, so long as the state did not "unduly burden" women's access to abortion: "it must be remembered that *Roe v. Wade* speaks with clarity in establishing not only the woman's liberty but also the state's 'important and legitimate interest in potential life.' That portion of the decision in *Roe* has been given too little acknowledgement and implementation by the Court in its subsequent cases."[47]

In an ironic (or strategic) twist, some conservative advocates argued that it was women's right to choose abortion that paradoxically affirmed the state's right to regulate and control pregnancy. John Robertson, a conservative legal scholar, refers to this as the "bittersweet nature" of women's reproductive freedom, which confers upon a woman the right to "bring or avoid bringing a child into the world," but also entails the loss of her legal autonomy from the time of viability and perhaps even from the moment of conception. The potential conflict between woman and fetus "gives rise to the seemingly paradoxical result that a woman has an unrestrained right to control her body until the fetus reaches viability and then suddenly loses this right once she decides to carry the child to term. At that point, if the well-being of the potential child is at stake, she loses her autonomy, and her body may be invaded and treated for the child's sake."[48]

Once a woman decides to keep a pregnancy, she gains a "duty to care" for the fetus and she gains responsibilities to insure the birth of a healthy child: "A woman is free not to conceive or, even though her actions destroy the fetus, to terminate the pregnancy altogether up to the point of viability, and she can terminate the pregnancy beyond the point of viability if its continuation threatens her life or health. Conflicts over management of the pregnancy arise only after she has decided to become or remain pregnant. Once she decides to forgo abortion and the state chooses to protect the fetus, the woman loses the liberty to act in ways that would adversely affect the fetus."[49]

What is the nature of her loss of liberty? Robertson's answers are quite clear. If fetal health were at risk, she could be forced to undergo surgery. If she were "mentally ill," she could be civilly committed. If she were an anorectic teenager, she could be force-fed. If she were working in a toxic workplace, she could be forced to quit her job. If she were a drug addict or alcoholic, she could be incarcerated simply for the "crime" of being pregnant and addicted.[50] Others have used the same line of argument to support the forced medical treatment of women (including in one case surgery on a hydrocephalic fetus in utero) and the mandatory confinement of women who abuse drugs or alcohol during pregnancy.[51]

From this point of view, it becomes clear that at the point of fetal viability, the woman's body can literally become the body of the state, at which point the pregnant woman might lose her most fundamental right to resist state intrusion. As Robertson explicitly put it, "she waived her right to resist bodily intrusions made for the sake of the fetus when she chose to continue the pregnancy."[52] A woman's freedom to control her body is circumscribed by the obligations she incurs to the fetus.

These obligations may be imposed upon the woman not only from the point of viability, but from the moment of conception. What if a woman engages in behavior early in pregnancy, like drinking or using illicit drugs, which clearly threatens fetal health? The Supreme Court's decision in *Casey*, with its re-emphasis of the state's interest in the promotion of "potential life," suggests that the state's authority may indeed legitimate such restrictions.

Fetal rights advocates draw direct parallels between a mother's duty to care for her children and a pregnant woman's obligation to protect fetal health from the moment of conception. As Phillip Johnson, Professor of Law at the University of California, Berkeley, argues in relation to drug-addicted pregnant women: "If a mother has a legal and moral duty to refrain from deliberately starving her infants after the moment of birth, there is no reason to exempt her from that duty during pregnancy. . . .There is no right to abuse children, born or unborn, in the third trimester of pregnancy or the first."[53]

In this legal and political discourse, women's autonomy is traded against (and often traded away) by women's right to reproductive choice. Such threats to women's autonomy have been vocalized not only by a small religious or anti-abortion minority, but by a wide range of liberal legal scholars. Alan Dershowitz, of the Harvard Law School, has also argued for the limitation of women's rights during pregnancy: "Now I am not a 'fetal-rights' advocate. I favor *Roe v. Wade*. I believe that a pregnant woman should have the right to choose between giving birth or having an abortion. But I am a human-rights advocate, and I believe that no woman who has chosen to give birth should have the right to neglect or injure that child by abusing their collective body during pregnancy."[54] While opposing the proposals of many fetal protection advocates, Dershowitz nevertheless adopts the logic and language of fetal advocacy to defend the restriction of women's rights, at least in the most extreme drug-abuse cases. A woman does not have the right to "inflict a lifetime of suffering on her future child, simply in order to satisfy a momentary whim for a quick fix." The rights of the woman are contrasted with the rights of the baby, or as Dershowitz phrases it, "Your right to abuse your own body stops at the border of your womb."[55]

Law as Social Coercion

By linking the maternalist affirmation of life with the masculinist use of coercive state power, fetal rights advocates have constructed a compelling case for fetal rights. In their view, the power of the state, through regulatory and civil law, through criminal sanctions and educational efforts, should be pressed into service in the great social project of "mandating respect for the dignity of the human unborn."[56]

Proponents of fetal protectionism clearly understand the coercive uses to which state laws can be put. As Parness states, "One major goal of the criminal law is to deter specific antisocial acts. Accordingly, criminal law utilizes the threat of punishment as a means of promoting proper social conduct. The aims of rehabilitation, education, and *retribution* are also sometimes served by the criminal law."[57] Statutes promoting respect for the unborn must provide "punishment that looms large in the minds of those who might act negatively toward the unborn. . . . The publicity accompanying the trial, conviction, and sentencing of criminals educates the public concerning the proper distinctions between good and bad behavior."[58]

One state attorney who has prosecuted women for fetal drug delivery has claimed that "the state's role in protecting those citizens who are least able to protect themselves, namely the newborn, mandates an aggressive posture."[59] Indeed, some child protection advocates hail a new age of "gestational rights," where courts can impose "medically necessary regimens" upon pregnant women or seek orders of confinement for women who commit "prenatal child neglect."[60] While such advocates acknowledge that such actions could be legitimate "only under the most extraordinary circumstances," they insist that "involuntary evaluation and treatment do occur rather frequently in mental health cases and cannot be ruled out in some prenatal neglect or abuse cases," even in cases where pregnant women are mentally competent by all legal standards.[61]

Such proposals are often driven by a sense that women now willingly violate the most instinctual norms of motherhood. As Phillip Johnson expresses it, in responding to an American Civil Liberties Union argument against the prosecution of drug-addicted pregnant women: "What seems to be implied in these statements is that a mother has a right to abuse her fetus in any way she likes, whatever the circumstances. Even animals have legal protection against wanton cruelty, but not unborn children.

Abusing them is one of the mother's American Civil Liberties."[62] Johnson argues that the decline of some women's attachment to motherhood grows out of the more general degradation of society's sense of moral responsibility. He wishes to grant to the law a kind of moral force in an effort to reinstate this sense of order: "Law cannot compel virtue, but the state of the law can tell us something important about the kind of people we have become. The crack mother prosecutions reveal a nation desperately trying one thing after another to slow (or at least protest) an alarming disappearance of personal and family norms of behavior that preceding generations were able to take for granted."[63]

The need to impose a "duty to care" through law and social coercion is presented as one symptom of a social order gone terribly wrong. While one may agree that pregnant women always have unique responsibilities, one may also believe that there is a greater risk in attempting to enforce these by institutionalizing coercive forms of state power. As Nancy Rhoden argues in relation to forced medical treatment of pregnant women, "It is far better that some tragic private wrongs transpire than that state-imposed coercion of pregnant women become part of our legal landscape."[64]

WITHIN this cultural context—one that perceives a fetus animated with life and victimized by the woman's neglect, ignorance, or abuse—public and legal tides began to turn against the rights of women and in favor of the rights of the fetus "housed" inside the pregnant woman's body. Indeed, much of the political, legal, and medical literature began to create a vision of the fetus as trapped within the pregnant woman, a victim of her excesses and freedoms.

The pregnant woman became the vessel which transported the fetus in its journey toward birth. The woman, in proper domestic fashion, houses the fetus, feeds it, and then releases it at birth. But a child that is housed by the mother can also be made homeless by her; a child that is fed by the mother can also be poisoned by her. The power of the pregnant woman to nourish and contain the fetus became a power that could be appropriated by others and used against her.

As the fetus gained ideological, legal, and political independence from the woman, it came also to be seen as public property, to be treated independently by doctors, protected in utero by the courts, and retrieved by the state, if necessary, after birth. The alienation of the woman's body from the fetus thus provided the grounds for the subordination of women's legal rights and the control of women's behavior during pregnancy by a whole range of social actors, from medical practitioners, lawyers, and bartenders, to husbands, employers, and agents of the state. These grounds provided justification for a range of fetal rights cases which arose during the 1980s and 1990s.

Public controversy over fetal rights extends beyond current legal discourse to endorse a public culture that generates more subtle forms of social control over women. The legal, technological, and cultural developments discussed here continue to generate attempts to cast women as unreasonable or irrational actors who ultimately are unworthy of the dignities, rights, and responsibilities of full citizenship.

2

Bodily Integrity and Forced Medical Treatment: The Case of Angela Carder

In June 1987 Angela Carder, a twenty-seven-year-old woman who was six months pregnant, was admitted to George Washington University Hospital in Washington, D.C., in the terminal stages of cancer. She had battled cancer since the age of thirteen and had survived chemotherapy, radiation, and the amputation of her left hip and leg. After three years in remission, she had married and become pregnant.

Aware that she might die before her pregnancy reached full term, she had agreed with her doctor to have a cesarian performed, if necessary, after her twenty-eighth week of pregnancy, the point at which the fetus might be viable. Because a major operation at this stage of her illness might cause her own death, she wanted to wait until she was sure that the child's survival was near certain.

During the twenty-fifth week of her pregnancy, she was diagnosed with a lung tumor and was admitted to the hospital. That evening, her condition took a turn for the worse and she drifted in and out of consciousness. On advice from her physician, she decided, along with her husband and family, not to have a cesarian section, which might hasten her own death and which the fetus would probably not survive—it had already been deprived of oxygen by its mother's failing condition.

The next morning hospital administrators learned of this decision and decided to turn to the courts for a judgment. The hospital might be morally or legally liable if it failed to attempt to save a viable life, they argued. A judge was brought into the hospital and separate legal counsel was appointed for the fetus, for Angela Carder and her family, and for the hospital. Carder's physicians testified that they opposed the surgery. Hospital administrators brought a neonatalist into the case, who estimated that the fetus had a 60 percent chance of survival. The court ordered the cesarian.

The attending obstetrician refused to perform the surgery without Angela Carder's explicit consent. The Carder family reported that she came to consciousness long enough to be told of the court order and responded, "I don't want it done." The family's lawyer called in an emergency telephone appeal, but a three-judge appellate panel upheld the court order, questioning the ability of Carder to make an informed judgment at this point and arguing that she had earlier agreed to have a cesarian performed at twenty-eight weeks' gestation. Another physician was found and on June 16 the cesarian was performed. Within two hours the twenty-six-week-old fetus died. Two days later Angela Carder died, having regained consciousness long enough to learn of the death of her child.[1]

The Carder family sued the hospital for violation of Angela Carder's civil rights. In April of 1990 the U.S. Court of Appeals released its decision in the Carder case, forcefully upholding the pregnant woman's rights and arguing that the lower court "erred in subordinating Angela Carder's right to bodily integrity in favor of the state's interest in potential life."[2] While defending women's right to refuse treatment, the court stipulated that "we do not quite foreclose the possibility that a conflicting state interest may be so compelling that the patient's wishes must yield, but we anticipate that such cases will be extremely rare and truly exceptional."[3] Within six months the hospital that had forced the surgery on Carder had issued strong guidelines defending the rights of patients to refuse surgery and had settled out of court a major lawsuit for damages brought by Carder's family.[4]

THE RIGHT to bodily integrity is so deeply entrenched in the American liberal tradition that when one first comes across cases of forced medical treatment of pregnant women it is difficult to imagine how such actions could be permitted under the law or justified in the public mind. The right to control one's body, free of state intrusion, is one of the most fundamental rights of liberal citizenship. To compromise this right is to compromise self-sovereignty at its most fundamental level. It is, in fact, to affirm a kind of slavery, the literal "taking" of a body against its will.

Under what conditions have such violations of bodily integrity been permitted? It might first be easier to identify the conditions under which they have *not* been permitted. Robbery suspects cannot be forced to undergo surgery in order to remove critical evidence, such as a bullet, from their bodies. Persons suspected of drug dealing cannot be forced to have their stomachs pumped if they swallow evidence. Suspected rapists cannot be forced to undergo involuntary blood tests for AIDS. Parents cannot be forced to donate organs to their children, even if the child's life is at stake and the parent is the only appropriate donor. One may not be forced to donate bone marrow to a cousin who is dying of bone cancer. Organs cannot even be taken from a cadaver without the prior consent of the dying.[5]

Clearly, the right to bodily integrity can be compromised only under the most extraordinary conditions. Even when the life of another person is at stake, as in cases of organ or blood donations, the abrogation of this right may not be justified. The Fourth Amendment to the Constitution guarantees "the right of the people to be secure in their persons, houses, papers, and effects against unreasonable searches and seizures." Even when this right conflicts with another's right to life itself, the courts have been extremely reluctant to violate this most basic liberal principle.

Contrast this clear legal tradition with the forced medical treatments imposed on pregnant women in the past two decades. At least thirty-six cases of forced medical treatment have been reported in the courts in twenty-six states.[6] Pregnant women have been forced to have blood transfusions against their will; they have been sedated, strapped down, and forced to undergo major surgery; they have been physically detained in hospitals when physicians suspected they weren't following medical orders. In 1982 a woman in Detroit went into hiding after being informed that she would be picked up by police and forcibly transported to the hospital if she didn't report by a specified date and time for a cesarian section. She gave birth to a healthy baby two weeks later.[7] A woman in labor in Denver, Colorado, described as "obese, angry, and uncooperative," refused a cesarian section when fetal monitors indicated that the fetus might be dying of oxygen deprivation (hypoxia).[8] She refused because of her own fear of surgery and her belief that the physicians might be wrong in their diagnosis. A court order was obtained on the grounds of child neglect and the surgery was performed. In two cases, one in Colorado and one in Illinois, pregnant women in their teens were forcibly detained by hospitals after they refused to accept medical therapy for diabetes.[9]

Despite the U.S. Court of Appeals' strong ruling in the Angela Carder case, thirty-five of the forty-six states that currently have living-will laws restrict women's right to die when they are both severely ill and pregnant. In twenty states, pregnant women are disqualified *without exception* from the right to die as soon as they become pregnant, even in cases where they have fully executed living wills.[10] Although in many cases these women, their lawyers, and their allies have been able to turn back attempts to enforce medical treatment on the grounds of fetal rights, one must also acknowledge that the forces which gave rise to forced medical treatment cases will continue to throw into question women's right to bodily integrity and self-sovereignty.

What could be the grounds for such interventions? That the woman patient is not mentally competent? The right to bodily integrity for pregnant women has been compromised even when they are fully competent by any standard, that is, when they are fully conscious, aware of the choices before them, and explicit in their refusal to be treated. Perhaps the violation of her civil rights is necessary to save the life of the fetus? Courts now often balance the fetus's claim to life in the last trimester of pregnancy against the civil rights of the woman. But why, then, is the fetal claim to life more compelling than the claim to life of a child in need of an organ transplant from a living relative or from a cadaver, or, indeed, a sick patient's need for the vital organs of a corpse?

On what grounds, then, have violations of such a basic constitutional right been justified? Clearly, some very powerful countervailing forces have been at work. First, as the previous chapter suggested, the fetus had to gain visibility and status as an "individual," with medical interests distinct from those of the pregnant woman. This led to the idea that the fetus might have "gestational rights," and that the physician might have separate obligations to the fetus as a "second patient."

But the individuation of the fetus was not sufficient. The forced medical treatment of pregnant women was possible only in a social climate which pictured pregnant women as either vindictive, ignorant, or irrational. While a man's refusal to submit to a medical procedure could be defended as rational, a woman's refusal to submit to a similarly invasive medical procedure for the sake of her fetus could not.

Forced medical treatment became possible only when the idea arose that women could no longer be trusted to subordinate their own interests to the interests of the fetus. As women moved more visibly into the public sphere, many people feared that women had abandoned the ideal of selfless motherhood for the masculine ideal of self-interest. From this point of view, it thus became necessary for someone else to be the guardian of fetal interests—a physician, hospital administrator, social worker, lawyer, or judge.

I begin with an examination of the technological and ideological developments that animated the fetus as the physician's "second patient." Next I examine the powerful narratives which have been used in social, political, and legal conflicts over forced medical treatment. Finally, I analyze the successful attempts to reinstate women's right to bodily integrity, looking specifically at the case of Angela Carder. This case suggests that it is possible to resist forced medical interventions and to reaffirm women's rights to individual agency only under very particular conditions—conditions that are more easily met by women of privileged race or class status.

Cases of forced medical treatment suggest continuing questions about whether pregnancy itself compromises or makes contingent women citizens' right to bodily integrity. Does the ability to become pregnant make women a different kind of citizen than men? Do they owe a deeper or simply a different kind of obligation to the state, one that may make their right to self-sovereignty less secure? If so, why is it that women's procreative ability, but not men's, obligates them in this way? Is this difference historically constructed—that is, is it an expression of masculine power?—or does the biological fact that women carry the fetus have some greater political meaning?

Fetal Surgery: "The Tiniest Patient"

In 1990, a team of physicians in San Francisco reported the success of a dramatic new form of fetal medicine: the performance of major surgery on a fetus in utero. "Baby Blake" was the first baby to be born after surviving major surgery while still in the uterus. He suffered from a diaphragmatic hernia, a hole in his diaphragm that allowed his stomach, spleen, and intestines to spill over into his chest cavity, leaving his lungs little room for development. At twenty-four weeks' gestation, doctors cut through the uterus, entered the fetal body under the left arm, pushed the organs back into their proper place and repaired the hole in the diaphragm with a Gore-Tex patch. Baby Blake was then tucked back in the womb to recover from his surgery. Seven weeks later he was born healthy.

Baby Blake's case marked the dramatic first instance of a fetus being treated as the physician's "second patient." Technological breakthroughs in the previous ten years had predicated this development, but never had the changing social and political relationship between physician and patient been so dramatically illustrated. News stories pictured the nine-month-old baby held high by his physician with captions such as "Daring Rescue."[11] The text proclaimed that doctors had learned how to "save lives by entering wombs."[12]

The development of fetal therapies carried a number of larger social implications. Such possibilities dramatically transformed the physician's view of pregnancy. Until late in the 1970s, pregnancy was viewed as an "immutable process that could not be disturbed or tampered with" and the pregnant body was seen as a "black box" that could not be "probed or opened without changing or destroying the very thing you wanted to observe."[13] New fetal technologies made pregnancy permeable, "manageable," in a way it had never been before.

The ability to treat the fetus directly also contributed to the idea that the fetus was independent from the pregnant woman, with medical needs and interests of its own. In fetal medicine, the physician was treating not the pregnant woman but the being *inside* her. As an article in the *Journal of the American Medical Association* characterized it, "In no other situation is the physician faced with one patient literally inside the body of another patient."[14] The advent of the science of fetology created not only a new view of pregnancy, but a whole new relationship between the doctor and the fetus, and by implication between the doctor and the pregnant woman. In the words of Michael Harrison, the fetus had clearly become "an individual with medical problems," a patient who "cannot make an appointment and seldom even complains," but who nevertheless needs a physician of his or her own.[15] In this unique relationship, the physician needed literally to pass through the woman's body to reach his second patient.

In some instances, the development of fetal medical technologies empowered women to make informed choices about pregnancy—to correct or treat problems with the fetus earlier in pregnancy or to terminate a pregnancy when the fetus was diagnosed with a serious problem. But these same technologies also held the potential to undermine women's autonomy and self-sovereignty by contributing to the public persona of the fetus.

As separate medical treatment of the fetus became possible, it came to be seen as imperative. The status of the fetus as "second patient" justified denying women their most fundamental right to bodily integrity, their right to refuse medical treatment, and, in the case of Angela Carder, their right to life itself. As long as fetal treatment remained voluntary and sought after by the pregnant woman, as long as it remained a medical treatment designed to serve *her* interests in the fetus, new fetal technologies were no threat to the integrity of pregnant women. But within a broader social climate which elevated fetal rights in the law and in popular culture, such technologies also had the potential to be used against women.

The Fetus as "Second Patient"

The visualization of the fetus through ultrasound technology made a whole range of fetal therapies possible. With ultrasound providing the visual guide, physicians could insert a needle into the uterus of the pregnant woman to remove amniotic fluid in order to diagnose genetic defects in the fetus, such as Tay-Sachs disease, Down Syndrome, trisomy 13, and sickle cell anemia. With the development of the "fetoscope," an optical probe with which they could literally see the fetal body, doctors could draw fetal blood samples and diagnose conditions such as thalassemia, a form of acute anemia, that could cause the death of the fetus before birth or illness and death after birth. Diagnosis of genetic disorders gave parents increased control over the outcome of pregnancy. In cases of untreatable genetic disorders, expectant parents could opt for abortion. Fetal medicine was welcomed by women at high risk for genetic disease, who had perhaps already experienced a stillbirth or had delivered babies who suffered and died shortly after birth. Fetal diagnosis quickly became accessible to a wide range of women as processes like amniocentesis became a routine part of prenatal care.

But the ultimate goal for those physicians pioneering the field of fetal diagnosis was not termination, but treatment.[16] In the early 1980s, before the advent of fetal surgery, physicians had experimented with less intrusive and dramatic forms of fetal treatment. In cases of fetal anemia, for instance, physicians could transfuse blood directly into the fetal abdomen, where it was absorbed.[17] No longer did the physician have to medicate the woman to treat the fetus, for now medications could be delivered directly into the fetal body. Obstetricians treated fetal goiter, which could obstruct the trachea and cause asphyxiation and death, by injecting medication into the amniotic fluid where the fetus could ingest or absorb it.[18] These less intrusive techniques for fetal treatment were more successful (and less controversial) than those to come. Unlike the fetal surgery on Baby Blake, such treatments posed little or no risk to the pregnant woman herself, except for the increased risk of spontaneous abortion or infection that accompanies any medical penetration of the uterus.

In the early 1980s, Dr. Michael Harrison and his colleagues at the University of California at San Francisco began experimenting with fetal surgery, inserting a needle directly into the fetus to shunt urine out of the bladder in cases of urinary-tract blockage or to drain excess fluid from the brain in cases of hydrocephalus. By 1987, the team had developed the techniques needed for full fetal surgery.[19] By 1989, Harrison's Fetal Treatment Program had received three hundred referrals, only seventeen of which met the criteria for surgery. In these seventeen cases, the average fetal age was twenty-four weeks, with surgery performed on the youngest fetus at eighteen weeks' gestation. The surgery itself took from ten minutes to over an hour. First, an incision was made in the woman's abdomen and then in the uterus, the amniotic fluid was removed and kept warm, and the fetus was partially removed so that surgery could be performed directly on its body. The fetus was then placed back into the uterus, the amniotic fluid was replaced, and the incisions were repaired. The major complication of such surgery was an increased risk of early labor and delivery. As the physicians from the fetal surgery team reported, preterm delivery remained the limiting factor "because successful correction of the fetal pathophysiology requires time for organ development in utero—the best possible intensive care unit."[20] In all seventeen cases, maternal outcome was good, producing few or no long-term effects. The major maternal risks were associated with undergoing two abdominal surgeries in one pregnancy (one for the fetal surgery and another at delivery, which was necessarily by cesarian section).

In some cases, surgery was performed not only to benefit the fetus, but also to correct conditions which might threaten the life of the pregnant woman. In the medical condition called mirror syndrome, the mother's body physiologically mirrors fetal problems. In the rare condition of hydrops, for instance, the pregnant woman may be at risk for cardiac failure if the fetus is not aborted or treated. Fetal surgery is thus used in some cases to treat both the pregnant woman and the fetus.

Despite the dramatic splash made by the Baby Blake case, successes in fetal surgery have been rare. All of the original seventeen women who underwent fetal surgery (including Baby Blake's mother) went into early labor. Of the first seventeen cases, one fetus had to be aborted and twelve others died at or shortly after birth. Of the four who survived, one is living with renal failure, one died in an unrelated accident, and two remain alive and healthy.[21] Despite these limitations, the survival of Baby Blake was perceived as a technological breakthrough. As one physician at the UCSF Medical Center stated, "Fetal therapy is here to stay."[22]

From Voluntary to Coerced Medical Treatment

Technologies for fetal treatment had implications far beyond their immediate application to fetal health problems. As the fetus became a separate patient in the medical and popular literature, the pregnant woman was transformed into a vehicle of fetal interests. The woman became the "maternal environment," the "operating womb," and even the fetus's "intensive care unit."[23] One actor is strikingly absent from the news coverage of the Baby Blake story: in the headlines, in the narrative, and in the visual imagery, the mother is simply missing. The survival of Baby Blake is neither her achievement nor her victory, for the story is not about her, but about the physician and his newest, tiniest patient.

Medical technology could now provide a number of ways to separate the fetus from the female body. Eggs could be removed and fertilized in vitro; the resulting embryos could be frozen for later use or transferred to the body of another woman. And now fetuses could have their own physicians and undergo separate treatment long before birth. Newspapers reported not only the extraordinary advances in fetal treatment, but cases where deceased (brain-dead) pregnant women were kept on life support long enough to "deliver" a full-term fetus. Women could literally "give birth after death."[24] The perception of the fetus as an independent entity under these extraordinary conditions contributed to the idea of the fetus as autonomous from the woman under more ordinary circumstances.

Public perceptions that the fetus had medical interests separate from those of its "host" contributed to the possibility that fetal and maternal interests could be opposed. Even as the physicians who pioneered the field cautioned that "because these procedures can be done does not mean that they should be done,"[25] growing public sentiment supported the idea that the obligations of pregnancy might include the subordination of a woman's right to bodily integrity, which she had presumably surrendered by becoming pregnant.

The development of medical technologies for the treatment of the fetus thus contributed to an atmosphere that made the coerced medical treatment of pregnant women possible. How were we to reconcile the "heroic" measures taken by some women and their doctors to save the fetus at earlier and earlier stages of development with the refusal of other women to submit to the most simple medical procedures, such as blood transfusions, to save a full-term, healthy fetus in the moments before birth? In the public eye, on both moral and legal grounds, the pregnant woman began to lose her right to resist medical treatment as the fetus inside her gained the ability (and, some argued, the right) to be medically treated. The pregnant woman was now cast as the person who stood *between* the physician and the "patient."

In the worst cases, the pregnant body became literally divided against itself as pregnancy progressed. Where before there had been one patient, now there were two. If the two came into conflict, there was increasing pressure to grant the fetus privilege over the woman. Particularly in cases where medical procedures could save fetal life with little medical risk to the woman, social pressure was applied on behalf of the more vulnerable, silent, and innocent "second patient," the fetus. The conflict between woman and fetus was not inherent in the technology, but was created by a social climate which increasingly came to see women as reluctant mothers, unwilling to sacrifice themselves, to subordinate their careers, or to suffer medical risks in the interests of their (born or unborn) children.

The reality was often far different. Most women with problem pregnancies were willing to endure tremendous physical and financial hardships for a chance to save the fetus. Demand for fetal surgery far exceeded the capacity at the UCSF Fetal Treatment Program. Physicians performing such surgery were careful not to place the medical interests of the fetus above the interests of the pregnant woman, rejecting procedures that might pose a risk to maternal health or a woman's ability to reproduce in the future. Yet the conditions which had made fetal surgery possible had also created an atmosphere within which other physicians, hospital administrators, lawyers, and judges could force women to undergo medical treatment against their will.

The Power of Narratives

Narratives provide a way for us to organize and understand experience. They establish accepted norms, they create social myth that helps to constitute social reality. Three primary kinds of narratives have informed debate over the forced medical treatment of pregnant women. The first kind portrays an explicit conflict between the mother and the fetus. In the public mind, these stories stand as a metaphor for women's rejection of motherhood and refusal to give birth. Women who refuse medical treatment to save a pregnancy that may have been unplanned or unwanted are cast as searching for a way out of a bad personal situation. These narratives characterize the women as bad or negligent mothers. Early reports of such cases first generated debate within the medical and legal literature over forced medical treatment.

A second set of narratives portrays women as irrational or ignorant. These stories characterize women who refuse treatment not as evil-minded, but as ill-informed. They appear as religious zealots, as unduly suspicious or fearful of modern technology, or as simply irrational in their refusal to accept medical advice. Often these cases involved medical conditions that threatened the health of the pregnant woman as well as that of the fetus.

A third set of narratives, ultimately the most important, depicts the pregnant woman's refusal of medical treatment in certain circumstances as rational and legitimate. The primary example is the case of Angela Carder, which resulted in a forceful U.S. Appeals Court decision upholding the patient's right to bodily integrity, an out-of-court settlement of a multi-million-dollar lawsuit brought by Angela Carder's family, and the establishment of guidelines by the American Medical Association and the American College of Obstetricians and Gynecologists supporting a pregnant woman's right to refuse medical treatment.

Bad Mothers: The Refusal to Give Birth

In 1979, a woman in her fortieth week of pregnancy, at full term, was admitted to the hospital in labor. She was diagnosed with a complication of delivery known as abruptio placenta, in which the placenta tears away from the uterus wall, causing vaginal bleeding and preventing oxygen and nutrients from reaching the fetus. Her physicians recommended an immediate cesarian section to save the life of the fetus. According to the reporting physicians, the patient "stubbornly" refused despite attempts by the doctors to change her mind. Two hours after her admission to the hospital, the fetal heartbeat ceased and a short time later a still-born infant was delivered. Before her release from the hospital, the physicians report, "The woman told a nurse that she was not disappointed and that the death of the fetus solved complicated personal problems." The physicians speculated that, as a thirty-seven-year-old divorced woman with two other children, she hoped to free herself from an unwanted pregnancy by refusing treatment.[26]

In 1984, a twenty-year-old woman was admitted to a hospital in Los Angeles in full labor. Fetal monitoring indicated that the fetus was in distress, again from abruptio placenta. The woman refused surgery. As reported by her physicians, "The patient was informed of the situation and told that for her welfare, as well as for that of her fetus, it was necessary to perform an immediate cesarean section." The patient refused to give her consent and stated, according to her physicians, "that if the fetus would die, it would solve her already-complicated life situation. This position was also supported by the male friend in attendance, with whom she had been living and who was not the father of the fetus."[27] The physicians decided to go ahead with the surgery against her will. No physical force was necessary to anesthetize her and a successful cesarian section was performed. After delivery, the baby was resuscitated without incident. Four days later the child was given up for adoption.

These early reports of maternal-fetal medical conflict represent the first set of narratives in forced medical treatment cases. The medical crisis presents the woman, unmarried or divorced, with a last opportunity to escape the obligations of motherhood, by abandoning the fetus in the last moments before birth. Her physicians are then faced with the choice of respecting her right to withhold consent and so implicating themselves in what they perceive as a "heinous process" or violating her rights in an attempt to save the fetus from imminent death or harm. Cast in such light, such accounts are deeply troubling and have provided powerful impetus for medical intervention on behalf of the fetus.

Dr. J. R. Lieberman and his associates published a particularly riveting discussion of several such cases. They suggest that most instances of maternal-fetal conflict can be attributed to the woman's irrationality or medical ignorance. But when her refusal cannot be so explained, they argue, "a suspicion of an occult reason arises"—"occult" in the medical sense of "hidden or concealed." The authors conclude: "It is probable that the patient hopes to be freed in this way of an undesired pregnancy and in no case will the patient share her *secret thoughts* with the physician. It may be undesired because it is an unwanted pregnancy, the woman is divorced or widowed, the pregnancy is an extramarital one, there are inheritance problems, etc."[28] They go on to make explicit the assumption that the woman is criminally intent on murdering her fetus: "The patient may conceal her *mens rea* (guilty mind) in different ways, and her alibi may be almost perfect, but the doctor's role is a singular problem. The physician does not have the opportunity to be neutral. He or she is either a passive accomplice, or is acting against both the patient's will and the law."[29]

In refusing medical treatment of the fetus, the woman becomes a criminal. She develops alibis to disguise her secret mission. If the physician does not intervene to save the fetus, he is an accomplice to the crime. The fetus is thus made to pay for the irresponsibility of the woman (usually unmarried) who, for secret reasons, simply refuses to give birth. The "unexpected maternal unresponsiveness" confronted by the physician is thus a cover for the woman's deeper, more insidious intentions. Under such circumstances, the woman's right to bodily autonomy may be curtailed by her criminal intent. She keeps the fetus "captive" within her body and this is the source of both her power and her culpability.

Incompetent or Irrational Mothers

In 1981, about four days before her due date, Jessie Mae Jefferson, of Butts County, Georgia, was diagnosed with placenta previa, a condition in which the placenta covers the cervical opening. Her doctor recommended a cesarian section, arguing that there was a 99 percent chance of fetal death and a greater than 50 percent chance of her own death if she insisted on proceeding with vaginal delivery. Jessie Mae Jefferson refused the cesarian on religious grounds, declaring that "the Lord had healed her body and whatever happened to the child was the Lord's will."[30] In conjunction with the doctor and hospital administrators, the Georgia Department of Human Resources went to the courts and won temporary custody of the fetus on the grounds that the fetus was not receiving proper prenatal care (although up to this point Jessie Mae Jefferson had obtained regular prenatal care). The hospital was given permission to perform a cesarian section when she was admitted in labor. The expectant parents immediately petitioned the Georgia Supreme Court to turn back the order, but were denied their request in a two-sentence opinion.[31] Two weeks later, when she went into labor, ultrasound revealed that the placenta had shifted and Jessie Mae Jefferson gave birth vaginally to a healthy baby before the court-ordered cesarian could be performed.[32]

In 1984, a woman expecting triplets was hospitalized in Chicago during the last trimester of her pregnancy. Doctors and hospital staff felt that the risks associated with a multiple birth required that they perform a cesarian section. The woman and her husband refused to consent to the surgery despite these warnings. Unknown to the couple, the hospital obtained a court order giving her doctor permission to perform the surgery. As soon as the woman went into labor, her doctor told her of his intentions. One physician who later investigated the case reported that when confronted with the doctor's intentions, "the woman and her husband became irate. The husband was asked to leave, refused, and was forcibly removed from the hospital by seven security officers. The woman became combative and was placed in full leathers, a term that refers to leather wrist and ankle cuffs that are attached to the four corners of a bed to prevent the patient from moving. Despite her restraints, the woman continued to scream for help and bit through her intravenous tubing in an attempt to get free."[33] The surgery was performed and three healthy babies were delivered. The woman never brought charges against the hospital.[34]

This second category of narratives suggests that women refuse surgery out of irrationality or incompetence. Lieberman and his colleagues suggest that "fear of surgery, prejudice, ignorance, difficulty with the language, or inadequate rapport between doctor and patient" are responsible for most cases of maternal refusal. They presume that the woman's fear of surgery is unwarranted and that her prejudice is based on lack of knowledge of modern

Western technology. Presumably, as well, the "difficulty with the language" is the patient's and not the physician's. In cases where "inadequate rapport" is the cause of the problem, we are led to assume that had the doctor better communicated the reasons for the surgery, the woman would surely have complied. The physician in one case ascribed the woman's refusal to have a cesarian section to her "ignorance and prejudice, which prevented her from arriving at an intelligent decision."[35]

The question of women's competence is a central one. Yet in most cases of forced cesarian section, the competence of the woman is never formally reviewed by lawyers or hospital staff. In none of the twenty-one documented cases of forced cesarian section analyzed in one article in the *New England Journal of Medicine* was the woman's mental competence assessed by a psychiatrist.[36]

Even when competence is established, it does not necessarily establish a woman's right to refuse treatment. In the Colorado case, for instance, a psychiatric consultant found the woman who refused a cesarian to be "neither delusional nor mentally incompetent."[37] The woman had given birth previously to twins and so was not a stranger to the delivery process. And although the surgery was performed more than nine hours after fetal distress was first documented by her physician, the child was born healthy. Her physician was surprised at the outcome and suggested that the case indicated the limitations of fetal heart monitoring.[38] In fact, in many cases of forced treatment, the physician's prediction of fetal harm turns out to be wrong.

Even in cases where physicians are certain that the fetus is in distress, the outcome does not always confirm the physician's judgment. Time constraints are critical: in most of the twenty-one cases in one study, treatment decisions were made within six hours or less, some in one hour, and one over the phone. The predicted harm to the fetus did not occur in six of the sixteen cases where outcome was reported.[39]

Another typical example is the case of a pregnant mother of nine in New York, who refused to submit to a cesarian section after her doctor informed her that the umbilical cord was wrapped around the neck of the fetus. The physician sought a court order in the case, but the judge involved refused to grant the order. The woman continued to refuse surgery because "nature makes these choices"; the baby was delivered vaginally without complications. The judge in this case, Judge Margaret Taylor of the New York City Civil Court, had refused the court order on the grounds that she "couldn't see subjecting her to possible death for someone who's not even born yet."[40]

Most women involved in such cases, it appears, have children already and are not ignorant of labor and delivery. In the first case study, most of the women (fourteen of the eighteen cases where age was reported) were between twenty and thirty years old and of the seventeen cases where reproductive history was reported, twelve had given birth before. All had sought prenatal care, most at the institution where the court order was later obtained.

Despite such reports, a number of advocates supporting forced medical treatment argue that intervention can be justified even when mothers are assessed to be fully competent. One child rights advocate, Donald Bross, in an article which explores the possibility of using child protection laws to protect "abused" fetuses as well, identified a number of conditions under which "prenatal child neglect" can occur, including mental illness and medical neglect. "Mental illness can lead to complete disregard of maternal health and consequent injury to the *prenatal environment*. Medical care neglect can occur—sometimes with fully competent mothers—when indicated medical procedures are refused to the probable detriment of the unborn child."[41] Evidence of neglect may warrant "intervention by child protection agents," including court-ordered "medical regimens" for the pregnant woman, court-ordered fetal monitoring (if necessary, by surgical means), and "involuntary confinement or restriction of physical activities" for the pregnant woman.[42]

Such suggestions mirror the recommendations offered by fetal rights activists such as Jeffrey Parness and John Robertson based on their claims that a pregnant woman has a "duty to care." Once a pregnant woman makes it clear she will carry the unborn child to term, Bross argues, "the court should be able to order her to maintain a medically necessary regimen." Failure to comply with such a regimen would make her liable to charges of child neglect at birth. Indeed Bross implies that a pregnant woman who is unwilling to adopt certain standards of prenatal care might have a duty to abort: "The mother may defy the court during the first trimester and decide to have an abortion. The child advocate would then be in the position of arguing that when intervention took place, the developing fetus had a right to die rather than to be born at extreme risk for deformities, pain or incapacity. That right would be of the same magnitude associated with adult right-to-die situations." In this way, child protection advocates could enforce the unborn child's "right to be free from willful or wanton disregard for his or her prenatal development."[43]

Standards of competence under the law are usually based on what a reasonable person would do under similar circumstances. While such a standard appears to be neutral, the question of standpoint is central: reasonable according to whom? From the viewpoint of traditional gender relations, it is clearly not reasonable for a woman to refuse to sacrifice herself for her pregnancy. A woman who refuses a cesarian section in the moments before birth when her own life and the life of the fetus might be at stake or a woman who refuses medical intervention on religious grounds cannot be seen as rational in the classical liberal sense. Almost all documented cases of forced cesarian section involve women whose religious beliefs conflicted with the dominant culture. How are we to measure competence and reasonableness in such cases?

The willingness of physicians to impose medical treatment is also deeply influenced by the race of the subject. In at least two reported cases of forced cesarian section, the women were African nationals.[44] In the case study of forced medical treatment, seventeen of twenty-one of the women were black, Hispanic, or Asian, and five of the twenty-one did not speak English as their primary language. In the two cases where women were actually subject to hospital detention (in Colorado and Illinois), both were young black women.[45]

Clearly there are issues of class involved here as well. Physicians in public hospitals have an easier time obtaining court orders against poor women of color than against wealthier women in private institutions. As one judge rhetorically asked, "Who would ask a judge to order Happy Rockefeller to have a cesarian?"[46]

A woman who refuses medical treatment is seen as irrational if she chooses to rely on the forces of nature or the will of God, rather than on the technological intervention of her physician; she is irrational if she trusts the medical establishment less than she trusts her own moral or medical judgment; she is irrational if she fears her own death more than she fears the death of the fetus. She demonstrates her rationality by a willingness to deny her self-interest and relinquish her moral decision-making power.

Bolstered by the ideology of the pregnant woman's duty to care, and motivated as well by the fear of lawsuits in cases where they did not act to "save" fetal life, physicians, hospital administrators, and medical legal counsel became much more inclined to compromise the patient's right to autonomy in the interests of fetal health. Despite the dubious legal grounds for such actions and despite, as well, the uncertainty of medical predictions of possible harm, members of the medical and legal professions began to lean heavily in favor of forced medical treatment. Concern about the growth of this form of forced treatment was sparked by publication in the *New England Journal of Medicine* in 1987 of the findings of a national survey of leading obstetricians and heads of maternal-fetal medicine programs. Almost half (46 percent) of the physicians surveyed thought that women who refused medical advice that threatened the life of the fetus should be physically detained.[47] A similar number (47 percent) supported court orders for forced procedures like intrauterine transfusions. Some 26 percent advocated state surveillance during the third trimester of pregnant women who "stay outside the hospital system."[48]

Troubling as well was that only 24 percent of the physicians surveyed consistently upheld a competent woman's right to refuse medical advice. Such attitudes reflected growing public sentiment in favor of the forced medical treatment of pregnant women. One Gallup poll found that almost 50 percent of the people surveyed thought women should be held liable for damages caused by refusing a cesarian section.[49] It was in this context that the case of Angela Carder arose, a case that would dramatically turn the tide of public opinion on forced medical treatment.

Women's Rights Reasserted

The death of Angela Carder and the subsequent lawsuits filed on her behalf marked a turning point in cases involving the right to bodily integrity. The decision by the Circuit Court marked the first time a federal court had heard full testimony in a case involving the forced medical treatment of a pregnant woman. The decision firmly established that "in virtually all cases the question of what is to be done is to be decided by the patient—the pregnant woman—on behalf of herself and the fetus."[50] The Carder decision led to the publication of guidelines by both the American Medical Association (AMA) and the American College of Obstetricians and Gynecologists (ACOG) which supported a pregnant patient's right to refuse medical treatment. The ACOG guidelines concluded that "resort to the courts is almost never justified."[51] The guidelines cast pregnant women who refused surgery as clearly rational and, for the most part, justified in their refusal of treatment: "the pregnant woman may decide that the risk is greater than she wishes to accept, or she may doubt the benefit to be realized." The woman who refuses to cooperate is presented as the rare exception to the rule: "the vast majority of pregnant women are willing to assume significant risk for the welfare of the fetus. Problems arise only when this potentially beneficial advice is rejected. The role of the obstetrician should be one of an informed educator and counselor."[52] These guidelines represent a clear turnabout from the attitudes presented in the 1987 physicians' survey.

The Angela Carder decision marked an important break with previous legal decisions. Most cases of forced medical treatment had been justified on the basis of two court decisions—one in 1964 involving a pregnant Jehovah's Witness who had refused a blood transfusion in a New Jersey hospital, and one in the 1981 Georgia case involving Jessie Mae Jefferson.[53] Unlike previous forced treatment cases, in this case the courts could find little reason to impugn the intentions or the judgment of Angela Carder. First, Angela Carder's commitment to motherhood was never in question; indeed, she had decided to become pregnant even though she was in remission from cancer. She had agreed, in consultation with her physician, to have a cesarian section performed (if necessary) only after the twenty-eighth week of pregnancy, when the fetus had a reasonable chance of survival. Clearly, here was a woman who wanted to give birth and had been willing to risk complications to her own health for the chance to do so. Her refusal of surgery at twenty-six weeks' gestation was based on the belief that there was little chance of saving the fetus and a great chance that the surgery would hasten her own death (which indeed it did).

In media reports, Carder was identified always as "Mrs. Carder" and situated always with her family in opposition to the hospital bureaucracy.[54] Her refusal of surgery was supported by her husband, her parents, and her physician. Indeed, even the medical staff who eventually performed the surgery did so reluctantly.[55] Whereas the Carder legal case was supported by a whole range of public health, medical, and legal organizations, the hospital was joined in its defense only by Americans United for Life and the United States Catholic Conference.

The legal defense of Angela Carder's case was based not only on her rights as a pregnant woman but on her rights as a dying patient whose last wishes were disregarded by hospital authorities. Thus the case was not framed as a conflict between the woman and the fetus, but rather as a question of the "right to die." No longer was the hospital seen as primarily concerned with the preservation of life, for it was now characterized by both the press and legal advocates as motivated by fear of liability and its own narrow interests.

In the wake of its legal defeat, the George Washington University Medical Center released new guidelines regarding medical decision making in pregnancy: "When a fully informed and competent pregnant patient persists in a decision which may disserve her own or fetal welfare, this hospital's policy is to accede to the pregnant patient's preference whenever possible." It continued, "it will rarely be appropriate ['rarely' defined as 'virtually never'] to seek judicial intervention to resolve ethical issues relating to a patient's decision or to assess or override a pregnant patient's decision."[56] Christine St. Andre, the Medical Center's administrator, stated that the new policy could help "keep these difficult decisions within the doctor-patient relationship" and avoid "the unnecessary and sometime detrimental resort to courts." She added: "George Washington has learned a great deal from this case."[57]

Indeed, there were a number of important lessons. In earlier cases the state had been brought in to reinforce the physician's power over the pregnant woman, but in this case the power of the state was turned against the medical authorities. In the face of this challenge physicians chose to retreat into the patient-doctor relationship. Recognizing this threat to their medical authority, organizations like the AMA, ACOG, and the American Society of Law and Medicine sought to defend their own base of power by defending the patient's right to choice. As the ACOG guidelines stated, "Clinicians should be aware of the destructive effect of court orders on the pregnant woman's autonomy and *on the physician-patient relationship*."[58]

WOMEN's right to bodily integrity has been upheld only under certain conditions: first, when the woman's commitment to motherhood is unquestioned; second, when the woman was able to align herself with powerful male organizations; and third, when the woman was able to "degender" the threat to her bodily integrity, that is, cast it as a problem not just for women but for all patients. These conditions are fundamentally class and race biased. Poor women (of any race), women of color (rich or poor), and women from non-Western cultures have had a more difficult time establishing both their commitment to motherhood and their rationality in the eyes of hospital administrators, physicians, and judges. Nor have they easily aligned themselves with powerful male organizations who might defend their right to self-sovereignty. Although the Carder case established an important legal precedent for all women, it seems likely that health care providers will continue to pressure women into accepting medical treatment, particularly women from these groups.

When the issue of forced medical treatment is cast as a conflict between maternal and fetal interests, the legal, moral, and political tide has run against pregnant women. When the issue is cast as a matter of the general rights of patients—and especially the rights of dying patients, such as Angela Carder, to have their last wishes respected—the tide turns dramatically against forced treatment. By "degendering" the issue and distancing it from the more charged grounds of fetal rights, the Angela Carder case was able to reestablish the grounds for the defense of women's right to integrity.

The defense of the right to integrity in some sense merely endorsed one sort of patriarchal power over women (the physician's) above another sort of patriarchal power (the court's). Nevertheless, this precedent should make physicians more reluctant to undermine women's decision-making power. Certainly, the dollar amount of the settlement paid by George Washington Hospital should give medical authorities pause.

Pregnancy and Citizenship

These cases make it clear that as the fetus comes to be considered an independent being, endowed with legal rights and entitled to medical treatment, women's claims to self-sovereignty, and indeed to liberal citizenship itself, will be deeply compromised. The right to be let alone by others, the right to be secure in one's body, is indeed more fundamental than any other liberal right and is qualified only under the most extraordinary conditions. There are far fewer exceptions to the right to be secure in one's body than there are to the right to free speech. When we tolerate even a single case of forced medical treatment for a pregnant woman—simply because she is pregnant—we affirm an entirely different standard of citizenship for women than for men.

It is also clear that physicians, lawyers, hospital administrators, and judges will continue to feel compelled to defend what they see as the best interests of the "fetal patient," particularly in cases where the pregnant woman is perceived in less charitable terms than was Angela Carder. Women who are different from their physicians in cultural or moral beliefs, skin color, or economic status are more likely to be subject to forced medical treatments. The Angela Carder case represents an important defense of women's right to bodily integrity. Yet perhaps the victory is less significant than the fact that the battle had to take place at all or the fact that the battle was fought and won on behalf of a white, middle-class woman whose maternal intentions could not be effectively questioned by higher authorities.

The cases of forced medical treatment examined here also suggest the deeply engendered nature of women's right to self-sovereignty, and hence citizenship. Women face a risk of social coercion never faced by men simply because of women's ability to carry a fetus to term. Certainly, men have been subjected to medical treatment against their will. Male mental patients and prisoners have historically been subject to serious abuses. But men have been vulnerable to these only once their claim to citizenship is compromised by some other condition, like criminality or mental illness, which might qualify *any* citizen's claim to bodily integrity.

The "taking" of the pregnant woman's body for the sake of the fetus might be considered equivalent to the "taking" of the male body for military conscription. But conscription of men is historically specific in a way that pregnancy is not. There are societies today that compel both men and women to military service. Additionally, while conscription is involuntary, it is compensated, publicly recognized, and actively rewarded by the state. Women who are "taken" for procreation are not rewarded for their "public service" (nor would we necessarily want them to be). The compensation received by soldiers (or their survivors) may be far from adequate, but even meager compensation has symbolic value as an acknowledgment of the soldier's loss of liberty or life. Pregnant women, on the other hand, are fully expected to accept their loss of liberty and indeed are punished for not voluntarily doing so.

The potential for state coercion is thus deeply gendered. Women are more vulnerable than men to state coercion, because of the historical construction of pregnancy, a condition shared only by women. As we recognize this essential difference in men's and women's relationship to state power, we must also recognize that pregnancy implicates women in moral questions and obligations that are not faced in the same way by men. Certainly, fathers have an obligation to contribute to the health and well-being of their children, and we might rightly expect them to provide support for prenatal care for their progeny. But feminists have also rightly made a convincing case for limiting men's involvement in pregnancy and in women's reproductive choices. Ultimately, for both biological and sociopolitical reasons, men's control over reproduction must remain limited.

What *are* the moral obligations of pregnancy? Although physicians and pregnant women may disagree over what these obligations entail, most pregnant women are willing to follow burdensome dietary regimens and other precautions to preserve fetal health. The most obvious way to protect fetal health, if indeed it needs protecting, is to ensure that every pregnancy is wanted and is voluntary. To attempt to enforce moral obligations by legal means, even in circumstances where the pregnant woman willfully and intentionally seeks to harm fetal health, is to endorse a kind of coercion that itself undermines any sense of moral obligation or responsibility. We can use our collective resources to cultivate a sense of moral community, but no matter how difficult the case the final judgment must always rest with the pregnant woman.

Faced with the potential for coercion represented by instances of forced medical treatment, feminists have been driven to claim that women, especially pregnant women, be treated the same as men—demanding for women the classical liberal right to be "let alone." Because the biological difference between men and women has been exaggerated and used to coerce women, it makes a great deal of sense to diminish socially constructed gender difference. But ultimately this position fails to recognize the particular needs, risks, and interests represented by the pregnant body. Until a new public agenda reflects and addresses these unique circumstances, the retreat into privacy for women will amount to a new form of disempowerment. Real reproductive choice rests upon recognition of reproduction as a social and collective responsibility, not simply a private and individual one.

For biological, social, and political reasons, the development of the idea of fetal rights presents risks to women's self-sovereignty that are never faced in the same way by men. These risks cannot be entirely diminished by transformations in the law. Nor can they be easily dismissed by denying the difficult moral questions raised by fetal development. A transformed public agenda must recognize this difference and address the distinctive ethical questions and social needs raised by the presence of the pregnant woman in the public world.

3

From Protecting the Woman to Privileging the Fetus: The Case of Johnson Controls

ELSIE NASON was over fifty years old and divorced when her boss informed her that a new company policy would require that she be sterilized or lose her job at the Johnson Controls battery production facility in Bennington, Vermont. The policy excluded all fertile women from the manufacture of automobile batteries on the grounds that low levels of exposure to lead posed an unacceptable "potential risk to an unborn child." Since women do not always know that they are pregnant in the earliest weeks of pregnancy (when, the company argued, fetal health may be most susceptible to harm), all women under the age of seventy at Johnson Controls were excluded from work involving potentially high lead exposure unless they could produce a doctor's note verifying that they were incapable of having children.

The United Auto Workers of America, the union representing workers employed by Johnson Controls, sued the company for sex discrimination on behalf of six women and one man who had been affected by the policy, arguing that the company was motivated not by concerns for health but by fears that Johnson Controls might later be sued if a child was born with birth defects as a result of workplace exposure to lead. Among the seven plaintiffs were Mary Craig, who had chosen to be sterilized in order to keep her job; Donald Penney, who had been denied a transfer in order to lower his blood lead level while he attempted to have a child; and Ginny Green, a fifty-year-old woman who had been transferred from her production job to a position washing the protective masks of the men who replaced her on the line.[1]

The Supreme Court ruled unanimously against Johnson Controls in March 1991, arguing that such a "fetal protection policy" constitutes a form of sex discrimination: "The bias in Johnson Controls' policy is obvious. Fertile men, but not fertile women, are given a choice as to whether they wish to risk their reproductive health for a particular job."[2]

BECAUSE public life has been historically defined in masculine terms, gender equality entails not simply integrating women into the public world on the same grounds as men but transforming public structures to reflect the needs and concerns of women. Women's structural integration into politics and work has been won only at the cost of that which made women "different" from men. In the previous chapter, the "pregnant citizen" symbolized the historical antithesis between (female) reproduction and the (male) polity: women's ability to give birth has been used to deny women their full rights as citizens. In this chapter, the "pregnant worker" symbolizes the antithesis between (female) reproduction and the (male) workplace: women's ability to give birth has been used in the same way to deny women full access to paid labor and economic independence.

In this social order, the pregnant worker is an anomaly in the masculine workplace, whose rules, norms, and physical structures assume that the worker could not (or should not) become pregnant. While the conflict between production and reproduction is most explicit for pregnant women at work, it is equally operative for all women. For some women, like Mary Craig, the conflict between work and family responsibilities meant sacrificing their very ability to become pregnant in order to gain access to good jobs. For others, it meant being silent in the face of daily conflicts between work and family care—shouldering the financial and emotional costs of a workplace hostile to care-giving needs.

The antithesis between work and reproduction becomes most evident when women enter traditionally male occupations. While women have gained access to such jobs in the past twenty-five years, the structure of work has failed to change to accommodate women. Equal access to work that is clearly still "male-defined" has not translated into gender equality. In work, as in politics and law, man is the "measure of all things." As Catherine MacKinnon has most forcefully argued, "Gender neutrality suggests, indeed, that it may be sex discrimination to give women what they need because only women need it. It would certainly be considered special protection. But it is not, in this approach, sex discrimination *not* to give only women what they need."[3] The challenge of gender equality is not simply integrating women into masculine structures of power, but placing what has historically (and biologically) been defined as distinctive about women at the heart of social structures and public debate in politics and work.

One risk of "going public" with women's private concerns is reinforcing essentialist assumptions about women's connection to motherhood, which entail treating them as if they were always pregnant (or about to become pregnant). Women's concerns about health and safety at work or about child care and elder care, or demands for flexible work schedules or parental leave, could also be used to keep women out of the primary workforce. The articulation of gender difference could be used to reinforce the idea that women were "secondary" workers and that work and motherhood were, indeed, antithetical.

There were risks, as well, that women would be subject to new forms of masculine domination in the process of raising "private" issues of concern to women. Worries about harm to fetal health from workplace toxins could be used by employers to screen potential women employees for pregnancy, to require that women already employed undergo regular pregnancy tests at work, or to monitor women's use of contraception or their "reproductive status."[4]

This chapter explores the paradoxical nature of public power for women by examining the emergence of fetal protection policies in the workplace. Central here are fundamental questions about how power operates in determining public policy.[5] Who has the power to define the territory of politics (what are appropriate and inappropriate concerns of the state) and to define the terms of political debate (how we talk about issues once they emerge on the political scene)? If the articulation of difference is essential to gender equality, then how we talk about difference becomes critically important. By examining how women transformed public power through political struggles over fetal protectionism at work, we can learn a great deal about the nature of state power and the risks as well as the advantages of "articulating difference" in the policy process.

The History of State Protectionism

Shortly after the turn of this century, the Supreme Court's decision in Muller v. Oregon articulated the justification for protective labor laws for women: "As healthy mothers are essential to vigorous offspring, the physical well-being of women becomes an object of public interest and care in order to preserve the strength and vigor of the race."[6] This line of reasoning laid the groundwork for contemporary justifications for excluding women, but not men, from toxic workplaces. The state's regulation of women's behavior has been based historically on assumptions of women's vulnerability to the hazards of the public world, women's inability to defend their own interests, and the underlying presumption that women, once released from private servitude in the home and permitted in industrial masculine workplaces, would not always place the interests of future generations above their own needs and desires.

Women's biological and social responsibility for bearing and raising children justified the state's special protection of women: "You know there is a particular interest we have in a girl. The girl of to-day is the mother of tomorrow. She produces our children, and we have got to preserve her a little better if we are going to have good future citizens."[7] Such arguments were used to support the regulation of the hours and conditions of women's employment at the turn of the twentieth century. Muller v. Oregon laid the legal groundwork for a wide range of sex-specific labor laws, from restrictions on night work for women to laws regulating the health and safety conditions of women's work. By 1924, only five states did not impose some restrictions on women's labor, restrictions which were not effectively challenged, in some cases, until the 1970s.[8]

Protective labor laws have taken many forms. Women have been prohibited from particular occupations, like lawyering, bartending, or work in mines and quarries. Women have also been prohibited from specific processes common to heavy industry, such as operating polishing or buffing wheels or working in the "core-rooms" (oven rooms) of iron, brass, or steel foundries. Pregnant women, married women, or mothers were often barred from specific occupations, like schoolteaching.

Early protective labor laws often restricted young women from occupations where they might compete with young men for jobs. By 1919 in New York State, for instance, women under twenty-one were prohibited from cleaning moving machinery; from delivering goods, telegraphs, or messages; and from work in any connection with elevated railroads, streetcars, or subways—even selling subway or train tickets.[9] While social convention kept young women out of jobs as apprentices in more highly skilled trades, state labor laws kept them out of more accessible occupations in less organized fields such as transportation and heavy industry.

Rather than excluding women entirely from occupations, protective labor legislation more often regulated the hours or conditions of women's work. In many states, laws prohibited women from working after 6:00 P.M., effectively excluding women from such occupations as train conductor and newspaper printer. Night work restrictions reveal the class and racial inequities of protection. Women could be restricted from night work as printers, only to pass on their way out the workplace door black women entering to scrub the floors of the building at night. Women could be prohibited from waitressing on the more lucrative night shift at exclusive restaurants, but could be employed as singers or coatroom attendants in the evening at the same restaurants. Women could be prohibited from working at night in textile factories, only to be sent home with extra sewing at night. Legislators rarely offered even the flimsiest justifications for withholding state protection from women who suffered the clearest threats to a "mother's health": agricultural and domestic workers.[10]

A remarkable range of defenses of protective labor laws for women was offered: Women were too vulnerable to the hazards of work. Overworked women made poor mothers and wives and threatened the health of men and children as well. Women were too ignorant of the hazards of work to defend themselves. Women were too poor to defend themselves, having fewer options for work than men. Either women "spoiled" work or work "spoiled" women. Women polluted "rational" occupations like lawyering with sentimentality or lawyering undermined women's capacity for motherhood. Women were "unorganizable" and thus needed the state to bargain for them. Or women needed to be removed entirely from the bargain. Gender ideology provided an infinite number of justifications for excluding (some) women from (some) jobs and leaving other women to work under truly exploitative conditions.

While clearly disadvantaging women who competed with men in professional occupations and industries, protective labor laws did improve conditions for women working in unionized female-dominated industries, like textile work. The nine-hour day was first established for women only. Health and safety regulations, like requirements for seating or fire codes, were often established for women first. Such legislation also laid important political and ideological groundwork for health and safety legislation for all workers by legitimizing the state's right to regulate the work-place.[11]

It was not until the 1960s that the accepted legal paradigm which reinforced the differential treatment of men and women in the workplace began to weaken. As more women moved into the labor force after World War II and as the feminist movement grew in strength, arguments for women's dependency, vulnerability, and need for state protection became more and more difficult to sustain. After the passage of Title VII of the Civil Rights Act in 1964, protective legislation for women only has been ruled illegal by the courts.[12] As the grounds for women's exclusion from men's work were weakened so too were the grounds for state protection of women. If women were equally capable of defending their own interests, then the justification for special protection disappeared.

Just as the specter of gender difference appeared to breathe its last, taking with it the basis for state protectionism, it was infused with new life by the powerful ideology of fetal rights. The rise of the idea of fetal personhood served to reconstruct and revitalize assumptions of gender difference, this time centering difference not on the susceptibility of women themselves but on the suscepti-bility of the fetus, which of course only women could carry.

The historical discourse of protectionism merged with the new ideology of fetal rights to place women on even more dangerous political ground, for now the state's interest had shifted from the protection of the mother to the protection of the fetus. As protective laws concerning women workers began to disappear, the fetus displaced the woman as the "object of public interest and care."

Johnson Controls and the Protection Paradigm

Why did fetal protection policies emerge when they did in the workplace? The history of Johnson Controls' policy illustrates the progress of fetal protectionism. Before 1964, when the Civil Rights Act became law, Johnson Controls employed no women in its battery production facilities, except in administrative or clerical positions. Under pressure from the federal government, Johnson Controls began hiring women in the 1970s. In 1977, the company instituted a voluntary fetal protection policy, warning all female employees of the risks posed by lead exposure and encouraging women "not to choose" jobs in which they might be exposed to lead. In 1982, the company imposed a mandatory exclusion of all fertile women from jobs in which lead exposure might be high and from all jobs which might eventually lead to promotion into such a position. The policy stated that "women who are pregnant or who are capable of bearing children will not be placed into jobs involving lead exposure or which could expose them to lead through the exercise of job bidding, bumping, transfer or promotion rights."[13] Johnson Controls justified its switch from a voluntary to a mandatory policy on the grounds that eight women became pregnant under the voluntary policy, despite company warnings.

Fetal protection policies have taken a number of different forms. Some companies, like Johnson Controls, have required women to prove their sterility before employing them in certain areas of work. Other companies simply restrict all "women of childbearing age" (as defined by the company) from work which the company deems hazardous to women's reproductive health. Eastman Kodak, St. Joseph Zinc, Union Carbide, Dow Chemical, Firestone Tire, General Motors, and Monsanto have all, at one time or another, established such policies.[14] Still other companies, such as A.T.&T. and Digital Equipment Corporation, restrict only pregnant women from hazardous work.[15]

In one of the most famous cases, in 1978 women employees at an American Cyanamid paint production facility in Willow Island,

West Virginia, were notified that they would have to prove that they were sterile in order to keep their jobs working in areas deemed hazardous by the company (where they might be exposed to lead). Five women underwent surgical sterilization in order to maintain their employment. Just one year later, American Cyanamid closed down its paint production facility for unrelated market reasons, dismissing all five of the workers who had been sterilized in order to keep their jobs. The women successfully sued the company on charges of gender discrimination.[16] Despite the controversy over this case, in 1982 the Johnson Controls company instituted an identical policy. In 1989, a federal appellate court upheld the Johnson Controls policy as non-discriminatory.[17]

Debates over gender-specific work rules now focus almost exclusively on risks to the fetus and not risks to women from hazardous work, casting them in decisively different terms from those of the previous century. A fetus may be vulnerable to substances that are safe for the pregnant mother, advocates of fetal protectionism argue. A representative of Dupont stated years before the Johnson Controls case, "When we remove a woman, it is not to protect her reproductive capacity, but to protect her fetus."[18] The validity of gender-specific labor policy rests squarely on questions regarding the existence of gender difference in susceptibility of the fetus to harm.

Making political hay out of the "gender equality" climate of the 1970s, early corporate advocates of fetal protectionism at work asserted that policies which excluded pregnant or fertile women were part of a continuum of efforts to modify workplace policies to accord with women's childbearing ability. Corporate executives argued that exclusionary policies were simply an extension of their concern for pregnant women and their children: "A child born with lead poisoning is tragic. To knowingly poison unborn children is morally reprehensible. Johnson Controls will do everything within its power to avoid having that happen at our manufacturing plants."[19] Armed with both scientific data and the morally charged language of protecting motherhood, corporate advocates of exclusion argued the fetus was extremely vulnerable to harm through maternal exposures. The scientific evidence, they argued, weighed heavily in favor of protectionism for women only.[20]

What made Johnson Controls a good test case is that the substance of concern was lead—a substance whose toxic effects had been studied for almost one hundred years, which had long been known to cause reproductive harm to both men and women, and which was one of the first regulated for reproductive toxicity by the federal government. More was known about the health effects of lead than about perhaps any other single workplace toxin. Lead exposures outside the workplace, including those from air, water, gasoline, and paint, had also been regulated by a wide range of federal agencies. Lead was recognized as a hazard not only to reproduction, but also to brain development in children and to the health of adult men and women (in contributing to heart disease, high blood pressure, and stroke).

Both sides of the case acknowledged that high lead exposures posed a serious risk to health of men, women, and children. They disagreed about the comparability of risk between men and women, a comparability thrown into question because women carried the fetus into the workplace. The heightened or additional risks posed to the fetus through the pregnant woman's exposure to lead was the foundation of Johnson Controls' policy. Questions about the "hypersusceptibility" of the fetus to risk were thus central to the case. Johnson Controls' rationale for differential treatment of men and women in the hazardous workplace was based on the specific risk to fetal health posed by the presence of women at work. The corporation's legal brief presented to the Supreme Court casts the question as one of balancing "gender equality... against threats to the health and safety of unborn children from toxic manufacturing operations."[21]

In an ironic twist, the Johnson Controls brief relies heavily on scientific evidence submitted by UAW witnesses for the plaintiffs in the lower courts. Risks from lead exposure are characterized in the kind of highly charged language usually reserved for industry critics: "There is overwhelming evidence that, at the levels at issue in this case, lead in a pregnant woman's body poisons the fetus's developing brain and central nervous system."[22] Because the fetus is "nourished by the mother, the unborn child possesses approximately the same blood lead level as the mother."[23] Citing depositions from UAW experts in the Seventh Circuit Court of Appeals decision, Johnson Controls argues that lead causes "substantial irreversible cellular and functional damage to the brain."[24] Harm from lead exposure may be clear and present at birth or may not become evident until a child begins school and "discovers that he can't remember, that his brain can't pay attention."[25]

The authors of the Johnson Controls brief report that the fetal brain is more susceptible to damage because it has not yet developed a barrier to toxins circulating in the blood, which are transmitted from the mother. Lead "binds to and is retained by an infant brain," causing devastating, irreversible, and permanent damage to the mental development of the "infant."[26] In addition, lead stored in the bones of the pregnant woman is released during pregnancy along with calcium to nourish the developing fetus. The immature fetal brain also takes up this contaminated calcium rapidly during development. Lead built up in the bones, blood, and soft tissue of the woman may be a threat to fetal health in future pregnancies long after a woman is removed from workplace exposure. It may take seven years for a woman's body to rid itself of this risk after exposure has ended.[27]

Key to Johnson Controls' case is the denial that the fetus can be harmed through its father's exposure to lead before conception. Fetal risk, the brief asserts, is transmitted solely by the woman. Although men may experience temporary infertility due to a decreased number of sperm (hypospermia) or decreased sperm motility (asthenospermia), birth defects or fetal injuries caused by deformed sperm (teratospermia) "occur, if at all, only at much *higher* paternal blood lead levels than those in issue."[28] Johnson Controls' policy excluded women from work involving maximum lead exposures of 30 µg/dl (micrograms per deciliter of blood); the company pointed out that hypospermia and asthenospermia have been detected only at 41 µg/dl and teratospermia only at 53 µg/dl, or "more than twice the maternal blood lead levels now known to pose substantial . . . harm to fetuses."[29] The "speculative" evidence of male-mediated risk is then contrasted to the "general consensus within the scientific community" of the "overwhelming evidence" that maternal blood lead levels cause "irreversible destruction" to the fetus.[30] The brief goes so far as to argue that science points to "no evidence of fetal injuries caused by male blood lead levels."[31] Damage to the fetus from the woman's exposure, by contrast, is "inflicted" at much lower levels because of the fetus's unique dependence upon the "maternal environment."[32]

Moreover, while adult male effects like "temporary reduced male fertility" can be individually monitored, controlled, and corrected by temporarily removing the worker from the exposure site, "such individualized monitoring of the effects of lead is impossible with a fetus."[33] Men's loss of fertility can be corrected on an "individualized basis without permanent reproductive injuries."[34] It is the "fetus's *direct* exposure to the maternal blood lead levels involved here that causes [fetal] injuries."[35]

Male risks are recognized in a limited way in some of the amicus briefs submitted on Johnson Controls' behalf. For instance, the National Safe Workplace Institute (NSWI) argues that "although lead exposure at some levels might very well damage both sperm and ovum, and thus cause infertility and perhaps birth defects, the biological fact that fetuses develop only in women means that there is another, qualitatively different opportunity for fetal injury when pregnant women are exposed to toxins such as lead."[36] The NSWI acknowledges that additional research on male risks is "urgently needed" and that researchers are "too quick to find hazards to women and too slow to investigate hazards to men," but asserts that current research findings on fetal injuries through maternal exposure are valid.[37] "We also cannot condone the [UAW's] efforts to downplay the tragic effects of lead on fetuses and children and to ignore the biological—as opposed to 'cultural,' 'mythical' or 'stereotypical'—differences between the reproductive functions of women and men."[38]

As with all of the briefs presented on Johnson Controls' behalf, the focus remains on fetal rather than on adult health: "This case . . . is not about health risks to the reproductive systems of women and men . . . this case is about the health risks to the brain and nervous system of developing children caused by *direct* exposure of the fetus to lead in the blood."[39] And this direct fetal exposure can occur only in women.

Johnson Controls argued its case on the grounds that *women as a class* could not perform the work as safely as men because women alone carried with them into the workplace the potential for exposure of the fetus to harm. As a related federal court decision put it, "the very womanhood" of the female employee undermined her capacity to perform the job satisfactorily.[40] Dr. Robert Klyne of American Cyanamid offered this defense of his company's exclusionary policy: "The ideal is that the workplace has to be safe for everyone—the man, the woman and the child. In the real world that's totally unachievable without emasculating the chemical industry."[41] Another corporate health officer put it more bluntly: "We don't allow children in the workplace and we shouldn't allow the fetus in the workplace."[42]

Johnson Controls rested its case on the following logic: Because the workplace cannot be made safe for fetal health, because women do not always plan their pregnancies (or know when they are pregnant), and because lead is a known reproductive toxin, the company has a responsibility to protect the health of unborn children by excluding all fertile women. "Johnson Controls wants to employ women. We have many in good-paying, responsible jobs. What we do not want is to put their children in jeopardy."[43] By couching the debate in terms of the protection of the health and safety of pregnant women and their children, major corporations, including Johnson Controls, had built strong support for their case from a wide range of people in state government, in the business and medical communities, and in some labor unions.

Maternal-Fetal Conflict

Defenders of fetal protection policies pose the debate in terms of the conflict between women's rights and fetal rights. As one chemical company association expressed it, "Since the fetus derives no primary benefit from its unknown or known presence in the workplace, it should not be exposed to excessive risks . . . This is a small price for mothers, potential mothers, and society to pay."[44] Another lawyer posed the question, "Does a fetus have an independent right, superior to that of its host mother, to require a workplace free from environmental hazards?"[45] The use of the term "host mother" is particularly interesting since it implies not only that the fetus has an independent existence, but that the business interest in fetal health may supersede a woman's own interest in the health of her fetus. It was through this "fissure" between maternal and fetal interests that employers and regulatory agencies asserted their right to protect the health of the fetus in the workplace.[46]

Johnson Controls' case made two implicit assumptions that questioned women's ability to make their own choices about reproductive health and fetal risks. The first assumption is that women are not capable of controlling reproduction. Women introduce an element of unpredictability into the workplace; the female body cannot be rationally controlled because women have unplanned pregnancies. This element of unpredictability is fundamentally disruptive to the workplace and has to be eliminated by employers since it cannot be managed or controlled.[47]

The second assumption is that women might be unwilling to subordinate their economic interests to the health interests of the fetus. The employer must thus act as a surrogate for the public interest, empowered by the state to protect the interests of the fetus when the "host mother" threatens to deny or neglect the interests of the fetus. An earlier court ruling upholding a fetal protection policy had likened the fetus to a "business customer" whose safety the employer had an obligation to protect.[48]

Thus if Johnson Controls was the responsible employer who "voluntarily" took action to protect employees and their "unborn children," then women workers were *not* being responsible. Johnson Controls could then claim that employers and not women workers should have paramount interest, and thus primary decision-making responsibility, for fetal health.

One reason for company intervention was the failure of its voluntary policy: "For years, Johnson Controls encouraged women capable of bearing children to voluntarily transfer out of high lead exposure jobs. This effort was ineffective as several women failed to do so and became pregnant while their blood lead levels exceeded the safety point for their children."[49] From 1977 to 1982 the company advised women of the dangers of lead exposure and indicated that they should voluntarily remove themselves from high-lead work if they thought there was any chance of their being pregnant. Indeed, as the lawyer for the UAW, Stanley Jaspan, argued before the Supreme Court: "The company went further, and had each woman sign a statement saying that she understands that the company recommends that she not work in that high-lead area if she might become pregnant."[50] Despite these warnings, in the last three-and-a-half years of the policy the company found that at least eight women with blood lead levels exceeding 30 micrograms per deciliter became pregnant (one of whom, the company claimed, had a child with learning problems as a result).[51]

But, as one Supreme Court Justice asked, why then exclude *all* fertile women? Why not simply exclude those women who clearly posed the safety risk—those who were pregnant? Because, Stanley Jaspan responded, "the employer is unable to determine which employees in the excluded class *possess the trait that creates the safety problem*. In this case, the employer is not able to determine which employees will become pregnant."[52] It is presumed, therefore, that all members of the class (women) possess the trait (pregnancy) that created the safety problem (fetal risk) unless they could prove otherwise. And, by implication, no man could possess the trait that could pose a direct risk to fetal health.

The State Interest in Fetal Health

Understood within the social climate created by the right-to-life movement and affirmed by a variety of "protectionist" government actions, Johnson Controls' policy was presented as a simple extension of established political precedent. Johnson Controls' case relied on the notion of conflict between maternal and fetal interests that had emerged in a broad range of fetal rights cases during the 1970s and 1980s. The Supreme Court Justice William O. Douglas, in another case, put it this way: "The interest of the mother and the fetus are opposed. On which side should the state throw its weight?"[53]

The assertion of this conflict and of the woman's "duty to care" appears most explicitly in the amicus briefs filed on the company's behalf by organizations such as the Concerned Women for America and the U.S. Catholic Conference. The brief of the Concerned Women for America actually refers to Johnson Controls' policy as a "child protection policy." Interestingly, the brief never challenges the right of women to work, nor even the right of pregnant women to be employed. Rather, it casts women's right to work explicitly in terms of "good mothering." The original purpose of the Pregnancy Discrimination Act (PDA), which made discrimination against pregnant women at work illegal, the brief argues, was to allow mothers to adequately support themselves and their children. The PDA "was enacted to help shield unborn children by providing suitable work and income for their mothers" and therefore should not be used "as a sword against the children by allowing them to be exposed to toxic hazards."[54]

Johnson Controls' policy does not exclude women from *all* jobs, "only those which expose their unborn children and future children to the industry's dangers."[55] Work is permitted, then, until and unless it conflicts with a woman's duty to her children, born and "unborn."

Citing the *Webster* decision as evidence of the state's increased interest in fetal life, the Concerned Women's brief argues that employers must now express the same concern: "it would be a strange anomaly that, as society and the law increasingly recognize the interests of unborn children, an employer would be precluded from doing the same."[56] The brief goes on to quote a case commonly used to support a pregnant woman's "duty to care" for the fetus: "justice requires that the principle be recognized that a child has the legal right to begin life with a sound mind and body."[57]

Another amicus brief, from the U.S. Chamber of Commerce, cites the many ways the federal government has warned against prenatal exposure to a wide range of toxic substances. Printed labels on alcoholic beverages warn pregnant women against "even moderate alcohol consumption which, although not endangering the woman's health, may cause severe birth defects."[58] The government has placed "conspicuous warnings" on cigarette advertising and packaging and has warned pregnant women against the use of illegal and legal drugs—even aspirin—during pregnancy. The Environmental Protection Agency has banned women of childbearing age from jobs involving exposure to the pesticide Ferriamicide, citing the likelihood of birth defects.[59]

Specifically in regard to lead, a whole host of federal agencies have expressed concern about or regulated lead exposure for the "unborn" and for infants and young children. The Centers for Disease Control have recommended that women of childbearing age not work in jobs that could expose them to high levels of lead. The Environmental Protection Agency, the Consumer Product Safety Commission, and the Department of Housing and Urban Development have all documented the tragic effects of lead exposure on young children from household water, indoor air, house paint, contaminated soil, and gasoline.[60]

A critical step in this argument is the analogy between children's health and fetal health. Federal regulations prescribed for the protection of young children are assumed to apply as well to fetuses (or to at least lend strong support to arguments for fetal protection). On this point, the Chamber of Commerce brief quotes a joint report by the EPA and the CDC: "Fetuses, infants and children are more vulnerable to lead exposure than adults since lead is more easily absorbed into growing bodies."[61] That the fetus is located inside the body of a woman is seen as irrelevant to the nature of the risk and to the manner of its protection.

Efforts to protect fetal health by excluding fertile women from certain kinds of work are presented by employers as consistent with a more general ethos of fetal protection. The employer is altruistically willing to place the public interest in fetal health before his corporate interest in profit and production, acting as an agent for the state's interest in the "unborn child."

The Responsible Employer

"In this day and age," Johnson Controls argued, "it cannot seriously be disputed that a company's desire to avoid direct harm to its employees and their families, its customers, and its neighbors from its own toxic hazards goes to the heart of its 'normal operation.'"[62] Johnson Controls thus casts itself as willing to shoulder its proper responsibility for the toxic burdens associated with its operations. The U.S. Catholic Conference brief connects environmentalist language with pro-life rhetoric, arguing "that employers be obliged to protect the health and safety of workers and the public, including those yet to be born."[63] Fetal health must rightfully become a "corporate concern": "Adoption of fetal protection policies is consistent with [Johnson Controls'] obligation to behave responsibly toward *all* members of society they affect."[64]

The supporting brief submitted by the NSWI defended Johnson Controls' policy specifically on these grounds. Health and safety should never be left to "market forces and 'free choice.'"[65] The Occupational Health and Safety Act, for instance, insists that employers "must be held *fully* accountable for workplace injuries and illnesses and thus must be given discretion to make safety and health decisions, even when those choices are contrary to the economic interests of employees."[66] Employees should not be free to sacrifice health and safety for increased wages, or be left to decide "how much workplace safety and health to 'buy.'"[67] For this reason, the location of responsibility must be shifted from individual workers to employers, and employers must, as a part of the normal operation of their businesses, take fetal risks into account in workplace policy.

The Chamber of Commerce brief argues that concerns about sex discrimination or about the loss of income to women workers should not lead employers to "blind themselves to the risks of birth defects caused by various substances."[68] As evidence of its responsibility towards women workers, Johnson Controls stated that it voluntarily agreed to "permanently protect the earnings" of all women who were transferred from battery production facilities because of its policy.

The fear of corporate liability, though downplayed in Johnson Controls' brief, clearly affected its policy. In oral testimony before the Court, Stanley Jaspan stated: "I think it is clear that employers, manufacturers, have now long been told that they are responsible for the consequences of their manufacturing substances. Manufacturers are liable, responsible, if they injure their employees, if they injure the children of their employees, their customers, their neighbors, and the environment."[69] Although no worker had successfully sued a company for in utero harm to a child, the courts' momentum in other liability cases signaled a significant risk to those who might be responsible for fetal harm. Indeed, the *Harvard Business Review* reported that the average jury award in 1984 against physicians who had injured infants was $1.5 million, while the average award against physicians who had injured mothers during childbirth was $156,000. A number of corporate giants such as the Johns Manville Company and A. H. Robins had been brought down by multi-million-dollar lawsuits over health risks during the 1970s and 1980s.[70] It would therefore be irresponsible of the courts, says the brief, to take the power to reduce liability away from the company.

Johnson Controls is thus cast as an employer which has done everything in its power to reduce the risks of lead exposure to its employees, but which is at a loss for alternatives to exclusion:

> You have a manufacturer who for years, before OSHA and beyond what OSHA requires, has provided extensive health and safety protection, lead protection, to its employees and the children of its employees. The company spends substantial sums of money low-

ering . . . the air lead in the plant through use of engineering controls, through use of make-up air units, through ventilation systems . . . We're not dealing with a situation where the company is
saying I'm going to exclude the women as a way of avoiding cleaning up the workplace. This is a clean workplace. But the acceptable lead levels [to protect fetal health] are so low as . . . agreed by all
the experts here, that it is impossible to do so.[71]

There is simply "no support in the record" for the argument that
the company is "male-dominated."[72]

Johnson Controls' case was strongest when it relied on the scientific evidence regarding fetal risk from lead exposure. Its concern about fetal risk was made even more compelling by evidence
that young children were more susceptible to damage from lead
exposure than adults. The case against lead was supported by
decades of environmental health research on the devastating
effects of lead exposure on inner-city children. The scale of vulnerability to lead exposure drawn by Johnson Controls runs from
adults (men and then non-pregnant women) at the low end to
children and fetuses.

But even if this scale underplayed the risk to male reproduction, the company's argument would remain compelling in the
public mind until a link was established between harm to male
workers (i.e., damaged sperm) and negative effects on fetal health
(birth defects). Concern over male infertility, even if it were
reversible, would certainly be warranted, but it would not compare to the social or medical concern that could be generated by
the risk of permanent damage to the brain and central nervous
system of the fetus. Implicit in the scientific literature was the presumption that damaged or deformed sperm were incapable of
successfully fertilizing an egg and thus transmitting birth defects
(an assumption known as the "all or nothing" theory). In the
absence of scientific certainty, cultural constructs of gender identity will color or substitute for science in evaluations of reproductive toxicity.

Despite the limitations of the scientific evidence presented by
Johnson Controls, the case does provide an account of the risks
faced by workers, especially women, in the modern workplace.
The available evidence warrants a great deal of concern over
reproductive health and the potential effects of exposing all

workers, and pregnant women in particular, to even low levels of lead.

The Power of Narratives in Johnson Controls' Argument

Johnson Controls' brief opens by framing the issue as a conflict between the interests of women—their desire for "gender equality"—and of fetuses ("unborn children"). The risk to the fetus is associated throughout the document with exposure to lead through "maternal blood." Lead in the pregnant woman's body "poisons the fetus's developing brain." The fetus's "direct exposure" to "maternal blood" is contrasted to the tangential relation of the fetus to the sperm of the "male worker" (not father).

This language implicitly locates blame and responsibility with the mother. The risk to fetal health is not traced directly to the toxin, lead, nor is it considered the responsibility of the employer. Rather, the risk is mediated by the pregnant woman, always called the mother, who delivers lead to the dependent fetus and who has, by implication, the power to stop the poisoning. The distancing of fathers from the reproductive process and employers from the productive process distances them as well from responsibility for harm to the fetus. The woman remains the primary site of responsibility and blame. Furthermore, the man can remove himself temporarily from the workplace to restore his fertility, but women's fertility is permanently damaged by her association with work. The more vulnerable woman stores the poisonous lead in her body, where it may pose a hidden threat to her future children. The risk is never characterized as a risk to the female body itself: the woman worker is never herself poisoned, but acts as a conduit, a "maternal environment," for others. Johnson Controls thus draws a narrow circle of causality and places women at the center of this circle.

The UAW's Argument

Opponents of exclusion begin by questioning the validity of scientific evidence used to "prove" that fertile women are the only conduits through which risk is transmitted to the fetus. The UAW argument and its supporting amicus briefs focused their critique

of Johnson Controls' policy specifically on the company's characterization of the reproductive process and fetal risks. Johnson
Controls' policy, they argued, assumes that reproduction is exclusively associated with women and denies that men may contribute, equally or at least significantly, to the transmission of risk
to the fetus.

Two related arguments were essential to the UAW's case. In
order to establish comparability of risk between men and women,
the UAW first argued that Johnson Controls had overstated the
risk to fetal health through maternal exposure: "At the relatively
low blood lead levels which Johnson Controls regards as sufficient
to bar fertile women, the primary risk is that the children born will
have 'very subtle' learning problems . . . The record is *undisputed*
on the fact that . . . fetal lead exposure at the level involved in this
case does *not* cause structural abnormalities in vital organs."[73] The
UAW was placed in the paradoxical position of diminishing the
fetal risks of lead exposure in the workplace in the interest of
establishing comparability of risk between female and male reproductive health. The ACLU's amicus brief states that "there is, in
fact, no basis for concluding that the fetus is entitled to a higher
level of workplace protection than workers themselves receive."
Fetal protection policies constitute an "irrational and inherently
sex-based approach to workplace health protection."[74]

Second, the UAW argued that Johnson Controls had understated
the risks to men and the risks to fetal health through paternal exposure to lead. The UAW brief drew men into the process of reproduction by challenging Johnson Controls' assumption that only
women could "deliver" risk to the fetus and by expanding the
notion of reproductive health to include harm to the male and
female reproductive systems before conception. The UAW argued
that the scientific evidence pointed to the possibility that male
exposure to lead at the levels established by Johnson Controls'
policy could cause serious injury to male reproductive health
and, by extension, to fetal health. The UAW brief quoted OSHA
standards on lead: "because of the demonstrated adverse effects of
lead on reproductive function in both male and female as well as
the risk of genetic damage of lead on both the ovum and sperm,
OSHA recommends a 30 µg/100g maximum permissible blood
level in both males and females who wish to bear children."[75]

Why, asked the UAW, should Johnson Controls focus so narrowly on fetal health rather than on the general reproductive health of both men and women—including damage that can occur before conception? By expanding the definition of reproductive health, the UAW position implicated men in the line of fetal causality. It challenged Johnson Controls' exclusive focus on fetal harm through "maternal blood" by emphasizing that exposure of men to toxic levels of lead before conception can lead to mutagenic damage to sperm, which then may be linked to birth defects or miscarriages. Men may also pass hazardous chemicals on to women directly through their seminal fluid. Studies of the wives of dentists, for example, have shown a higher miscarriage rate due to the exposure of their husbands to anesthetic gases.[76] The company's executives, an amicus brief argued, failed to consider "the children who are desperately wanted but never get conceived. They are less likely to think about the miscarriages suffered by a wife of a male worker because his sperm was damaged by lead exposure. But to the families who must live with the consequences of lead, the infertility or the pregnancy loss may be more of a tragedy . . . than a wanted child who turns out to be less intelligent or capable than some of her peers."[77] The company's facile dismissal of the risk to reproductive health through the male system makes this policy look as if it "has little to do with fetal protection and a lot to do with sex discrimination."[78]

The link between scientific knowledge and politics is made clear, according to the UAW, when we examine how standards of scientific proof are deeply biased to favor recognition of some kinds of health effects (direct fetal harm through maternal exposure) over others (general reproductive harm to both men and women). Scientific standards of proof are more strict for male-mediated risks than for female-mediated risks. Scientific studies have assumed female vulnerability and male invulnerability and have often therefore left men entirely out of research or have controlled poorly for fathers' exposures. Studies assume, for instance, that a damaged egg can still be fertilized (indeed, in some cases, be more vulnerable to penetration by the sperm), but that damaged sperm are incapable of penetrating an egg.

The amicus brief from the American Public Health Association reports instead that "sperm studies may act as a kind of early warning system for reproductive risk"[79] and that NIOSH recommends studies of semen quality to "help identify workplaces where some types of hazards to reproduction exist, preferably before irreversible testicular damage or other profound disorders of reproduction occur."[80] Fathers' exposure to radiation has been linked to childhood cancer, and paternal exposure to lead has been associated with "disastrous" nervous disorders.[81]

Indeed, a different interpretation of the available data might be that men are *more* susceptible to harm than women. Men's reproductive organs are on the outside of the body, making them more vulnerable to heat and caustic exposures, and sperm are some of the smallest and most vulnerable cells in the body.[82] Men are also at risk for longer periods during their lives because they may procreate for many more years than women. In a different social order, the existing medical evidence could be used to exclude *men* from toxic workplaces.

The Politics of Science

The Seventh Circuit Court of Appeals upheld Johnson Controls' policy as nondiscriminatory on the grounds that the evidence of male-mediated effects on fetal health was "at best, speculative and unconvincing." In the court's words, "The UAW's animal research evidence does not present the type of solid scientific data necessary for a reasonable factfinder to reach a non-speculative conclusion that a father's exposure to lead presents the same danger to the unborn child as that resulting from a female employee's exposure to lead."[83] Because harm to the "unborn child" is "substantially confined to female employees," the selective exclusion of women from production is held not to be discriminatory, but rather to be based on scientific evidence of biological difference.

There are two basic ways that fetal health can be harmed by toxic substances. First, toxins may cause mutations in the genetic structure of sperm and egg cells before conception (mutagenesis). While the effects of mutagens may not be readily apparent as the fetus develops in utero, they may be dramatic after birth, causing childhood cancers or congenital heart problems, for instance. This kind of harm can occur through either male or female exposure.

Second, fetal health can be harmed by direct exposure to a toxic substance after conception, damaging the fetus as it develops in utero (teratogenesis). Just as adults can be poisoned by toxins, the fetus may be harmed by substances which cross over the placenta and harm the fetus as it develops. This kind of harm can occur only through the pregnant woman.[84]

Johnson Controls' policy (and the Seventh Circuit decision) focused exclusively on the second kind of effect (through the pregnant woman) while dismissing the first kind of effect (through both male and female). Male-mediated mutagenic effects were documented primarily on the basis of animal studies, while female-mediated teratogenic effects were based on human epidemiological studies. Science and not gender assumptions presumably drove them to the conclusion that exposures to the woman presented a more substantial—in fact, a unique and exclusive—risk to fetal health.

The amicus brief submitted by the National Resources Defense Council draws a contrary conclusion. In order to uphold Johnson Controls' position, it would be necessary to defend two fundamental assumptions. First, one would have to argue that the effects of preconception exposure to toxins were less potentially damaging or significant to fetal health than postconception exposure. That is, there would have to be scientific reason to believe that mutagens posed less harm to fetal health than teratogens. Second, one would have to argue that animal studies were a weaker predictor of harm to fetal health than human epidemiological studies. The Seventh Circuit decision based its argument on the greater strength of the epidemiological studies.

The NRDC brief challenged both assumptions. "It cannot be said that one effect is more significant than the other ... Exposure to one chemical may present a high probability of a relatively modest consequence (e.g., slightly reduced I.Q.) while exposure to another chemical may pose a low probability of a disastrous consequence (e.g., hydrocephalus)."[85] In addition, "exposure to a single substance may pose a risk of both kinds of adverse effects. Preconception exposure of either the male or female may pose a small probability of mutation leading to a grotesque malformity, while post-conception exposure of the female may lead to more modest health effects."[86]

Both sides agreed that the postconception exposures were relatively well understood and well documented in human studies, animal studies, and clinical observations.[87] But male-mediated effects, because they occur before conception, are more likely to be documented through animal studies. It is much more difficult to document preconception effects through human studies. Epidemiological studies of mutagens would have to take into account male and female exposures long before conception, as well as all of the "confounding" factors (nutrition, smoking, drug and alcohol use, and so on) which may affect reproduction as well. Such studies would have to account for spontaneous abortions caused by mutagenic substances as well as pregnancies that went to full term. The difficulty of isolating the effects of a single mutagen in human studies has forced federal agencies to rely heavily on controlled animal studies as the basis for regulatory standards. Some scientists have argued for the superiority of animal studies, precisely because confounding factors are easier to control.[88]

The NRDC brief asserted that "reliance on animal studies is concededly more 'speculative,' but it is wrong for the court to conclude that animal studies are not 'convincing' or 'solid' scientific data."[89] In fact, the court's assumption goes against the standards of scientific certainty established by federal agencies and the courts: "Virtually every other federal agency charged with protecting the public health for hazardous chemicals has also extrapolated from 'mouse to man' in evaluating human health risks. Indeed, it would be irresponsible for an agency charged with protecting health to do otherwise."[90] Animal studies are the central, and sometimes the only, source of data for federal regulations concerning cancer-causing substances in pesticides and insecticides, in polluted water and air, and in consumer goods.[91]

The NRDC goes on to say that the Johnson Controls position represents a "callous indifference" to the reproductive health of men. The failure to consider animal studies, another amicus brief argues, is "tantamount to saying to men, 'Many of you will have to become sterile, many of you will have to suffer through your wives' miscarriages, many of you will have to shoulder the burden of damaged children, until such time as medical science produces more studies of men and conclusive studies of men.'"[92]

Johnson Controls' policy, therefore, can be considered "scientifically irrational."[93]

The underlying bias of fetal protectionism becomes apparent when one looks at how the business community and the state have dealt with known male reproductive hazards. When the chemical DBCP was discovered to cause infertility in men working in a chemical company in California in 1977, the company was immediately shut down and a ban on further use of the substance was imposed. The chemical, not the men, was removed from the production process.[94] By contrast, in the same year the Bunker Hill Co. of Idaho required that women working with known reproductive hazards prove they were sterile before permitting them to keep their jobs.[95]

Knowledge of male reproductive hazards has not always led to the protection of men. On the contrary, in most companies the exclusive focus on pregnant women has led to a complete lack of attention to male hazards. Some analysts have suggested that the lack of concern over male exposures is due to the difficulty involved in lawsuits brought by fathers of affected children, because fathers have to prove paternity before proving that reproductive disorders resulted from work-related exposures.[96]

Including men in the discussion of reproductive processes was the first strategy used by the UAW to discount the exclusive focus on maternal exposure. The second strategy was to collapse the distinction between reproductive risks and other kinds of risks to adult health, as in this statement from the Trial Lawyers brief: "The company's assertions of 'moral concern' for fetal health are severely undermined by the risks to employee and consumer health that Johnson Controls routinely creates and tolerates." The UAW brief adds that lead exposure at very low levels also causes a wide range of serious health problems for adult men and women, including increased risk of high blood pressure, heart disease, stroke, and neurological damage.

Why does the company discount risks like cardiovascular damage to men from exposures as low as 10 µg/dl of lead? Why does it tolerate the environmental risks to the community from disposal of old batteries, or the risks to older children from lead dust brought home on workers' clothing? In light of these inconsistencies, the UAW characterized Johnson Controls' use of science as a "disingenuous rationalization" for reducing corporate liability and keeping women out of well-paying jobs. An exclusive focus on fetal health, or even on reproductive health, cannot be justified, the brief argues, by the scientific evidence on health risks from lead.

Engendered Difference

Johnson Controls' standards of proof for male-mediated reproductive effects differed from standards of proof for female-mediated effects (or even from standards of carcinogenicity) because company policy was informed not by science but by engendered cultural assumptions about men, women, work, and reproduction. Explicit historical ties can be drawn to the logic underlying the 1908 U.S. Supreme Court decision in Muller v. Oregon, which established a maximum hour law for women on the grounds of their greater vulnerability to the hazards and stresses of the workplace. Following the *Muller* precedent, Johnson Controls attempted to legitimate its policy by submerging its cultural claims about women's exclusive relation to motherhood under the cover of "scientific knowledge" of difference between the sexes.

Like their historical sisters who opposed gender-specific protective labor legislation, opponents of exclusion argue that women as a class pay too high a price for protection. Anecdotal evidence suggests that some women face demotion or dismissal when they become pregnant. Women working in microchip production, for instance, often lose their jobs if the company cannot find "suitable" work for them while they are pregnant. This means not only loss of pay, but loss of health insurance in the middle of a pregnancy. One study of a chemical company reports that women's wages dropped dramatically and women workers lost all seniority benefits after an exclusionary policy was instituted.[97] A woman who had been faced with the choice between sterilization and loss of her job stated, "It seemed that you could have a tubal ligation in a very short period of time. It cost about $800 and it seemed to be less than what one would pay for an employment agency to find you a job!"[98]

If scientific concern for fetal health did not drive Johnson Controls' policy, then cultural assumptions about women, work, and motherhood surely did. Johnson Controls' policy was initiated by the company physician, Charles Fishburn, who had testified in a Seventh Circuit deposition that he had always believed that women should not be assigned to jobs that involved lead exposure: "For medical legal reasons, as a knowledgeable physician I must take this position in order to protect the unborn child from the pressures of society. I feel that regardless of the sophistication of man-made laws the physician still must abide by the laws governing the natural environment and the laws of nature."[99] Briefs for the UAW portray a company motivated not by the universal public interest in the protection of health, but by the particular concerns of bosses holding stereotypical assumptions about women, obsessed with their own liability, and unwilling to make the changes necessary to fully and equally integrate women into a traditionally male workplace.

Indeed, internal company memos implicitly recognized that the policy might, instead of "protecting" motherhood, lead women to sacrifice motherhood (by getting sterilized in order to keep their jobs). The company recognized as well that the policy would lead to the exclusion of women from jobs targeted by affirmative action policies. Johnson Controls' policy presented women with a trade-off between their work and their ability to become mothers. It said, essentially: To enter here you must leave at the door that which makes you women. The company recognized the possibility that its policy could lead women to be literally sterilized, that is, stripped of that which makes them different from men.

An internal company memo outlining the fetal protection policy states that "it is in no way intended to support or encourage women of childbearing capability to seek to change this status."[100] In another memo, the company recognizes that women will seriously consider this option and directs managers to discourage them from choosing it: "If, in your contacts with the employee, you sense that the employee is contemplating sterilization it is expected that you would counsel against such a procedure for the sake of avoiding action under the Fetal Protection Program."[101] Questions regarding sterilization (which the authors of the memo anticipate will come from both women workers and new applicants) should be "referred to the Nurse."[102]

Company documents also recognize that the fetal protection policy would naturally lead to the employment of fewer women in traditionally male jobs targeted by affirmative action and equal employment opportunity plans: "From an 'AAP' [Affirmative Action Program] and 'EEO' [Equal Employment Opportunity] point of view... AAP's should be reviewed in light of this policy. It is anticipated that commitments regarding plant female hiring will be significantly lower in the future."[103]

The company recognizes, as well, that it is no longer acceptable in the public mind (and in the law) simply to ban women who are capable of childbearing from employment: "From a 'PR' point of view, we are *not* saying that we have discontinued hiring fertile females. We *are* saying that hiring is restricted as specified in the policy." Contrast this to the next directive to plant managers concerning "applicant flow procedures": "Perhaps the most practical procedure regarding applicants would be to ask your plant contact point (receptionist?) to inform female applicants that 'we have no openings for women capable of bearing children at this time.'"[104]

Race, Class, and the Sexual Division of Labor

Amicus briefs for the UAW make a compelling case for arguments that such gender-specific policies are feasible only in workplaces where women are in the minority and can be easily replaced by men. The UAW's brief pointed out that "fertile women are not likely to be excluded wholesale from jobs as childcare workers, nurses, or dental assistants, among other examples, even though those jobs involve exposure to fetal hazards."[105]

Protection is an illusion, because its application is skewed by gender, race, and class. Hospital workers, for example, work with known reproductive hazards such as ethylene oxide (used to sterilize equipment), radiation, chemotherapeutic drugs, and anesthetic gases, yet they are not subject to exclusionary policies as a class. African-American women are disproportionately employed in the health care industry and in the most hazardous positions, such as that of nurse's aide, where little concern is expressed for women's reproductive health.

The focus on fetal protectionism must also be placed in the context of the general disregard for health of women (and men) of color in the workplace. One study of laundry and drycleaning workers found that African-American male and female workers had death rates, from all causes, double that of white workers, and that African-Americans in general have higher death rates from cancer of the liver, lung, cervix, uterus, and skin.[106]

Migrant farmworkers, predominantly Chicano and African-American, have a life expectancy *twenty years* less than the national average: "Their exposure to pesticides, heat, mechanical hazards, noise and dust, combine with poverty and poor medical care to lower the life expectancy of a farmworker to 49 years."[107] Women farmworkers—especially migrant workers—are also constantly exposed to pesticides which are known carcinogens and teratogens.[108] Women assembly-line workers in the electronics industry encounter acids, solvents, and radiation, with little corporate concern for their health. Where women compete with men, they may be excluded; where they remain in traditionally female occupations or in poor-paying jobs, they receive little or no protection at all.

Finally, advocates of a more equitable approach argue that what fetal protection policies protect best is corporate economic interests. By excluding women from hazardous jobs, companies have opted to risk discrimination suits rather than tort liabilities for miscarriages or birth defects. As one corporate lawyer put it, "It was easier to deal with union protests over the exclusion of women than with a damage trial in 1990 where a jury would be confronted by a horribly deformed human being."[109] As the number of women in heavy industries increases and as knowledge of female reproductive hazards expands, the practice of exclusion may become more widespread.

Advocates of equity support a safer workplace for all workers, rather than one which focuses so exclusively on the risks to fetal health. One alternative is gender-neutral policies which protect all "potential parents" in the workplace (and hence protect fetuses as well). Policies which exclude pregnant women from the workplace remove the incentive for corporations to eliminate hazards by removing the threat of lawsuits, at a low cost to employers. The cost to women employees is much higher; as Joan Bertin of the

ACLU writes, "The price of safety cannot be the loss of civil and constitutional rights."[110]

Irresponsible Mothers

The UAW's case addressed the deeper gender assumptions underlying fetal protection policies. It predicted that the net effect of fetal protection policies would be "to permit employers to exclude all fertile women from almost all nonsedentary jobs."[111] These policies would result in what the UAW refers to as a "parade of horribles" for women. The consequences are laid out in the brief submitted by the Trial Lawyers for Justice: "There is no logical line at which to end acceptance of professed concerns for fetal health. Just as lead and other toxins may pose a risk to fetuses, so may stress, fatigue, standing or sitting for long hours, and exposure to the colds, viruses, and cigarette smoke of other workers."[112] Should employers have the right to exclude women from any work that exposes them to such "hazards"? "Should taxi and bus companies be able to refuse to hire women as drivers because, if they got pregnant and if they were in an accident, it would be not only them but their fetuses that might be injured?"[113]

The Trial Lawyers brief characterized their opponent's argument this way: "All of the professed 'moral concern' about fetal health boils down to the following chain of reasoning: because women can get pregnant, and because some of them *might* get pregnant, and some of these who get pregnant *might* have high blood lead levels, and then perhaps some of the children born to these women *might* have some developmental problems, in order to avoid this slight possibility, we must refuse to hire *all* women who are physically capable of bearing children."[114] The UAW argued effectively that such a policy is overinclusive. For women, "the birth rate is near zero at age 40, with only a .41 percent probability that a woman between the ages of 40 and 44 will give birth," and almost no probability that a woman aged 45–49 will give birth. "Moreover, four out of five sexually active, fertile women not seeking pregnancy use contraceptives."[115]

Exclusionary policies assume that women will not voluntarily control their reproduction and will not place the interests of fetal health before their own economic interests. They assume as well that employers will take account of fetal health more rationally than women workers themselves. Underlying these assumptions is a moral judgment about who is best positioned to protect and defend the health of "unborn children." As the New York Bar brief put it, "it is both irrational and counterproductive, from a public health point of view, to pit woman against fetus, as though their interests were adverse. Women who want children want healthy fetuses and often take great risks to ensure the well-being of their future children...The suggestion that employers may properly substitute their judgment for a woman's when it comes to the care of her potential offspring or her need for employment, is both humiliating and insulting to women."[116]

Even if Johnson Controls could produce a woman who had disregarded fetal health to advance herself economically, even if they could prove that women could not control reproduction well enough to diminish risks to the fetus, the UAW argued, it would indeed be discriminatory to assume that what was true for some women, or even most women, would be true for *all* women. As the Supreme Court had ruled in L.A. Department of Water and Power v. Manhart, a "true generalization about the class is insufficient reason for disqualifying an individual to whom the generalization may not apply."[117]

Still, the question of women's rationality and their ability to make responsible choices about fetal health lies at the heart of this debate. Beyond assuming that all women are likely to become pregnant, and that reproduction is exclusively female, Johnson Controls' policy assumes as well that women are incapable of making "autonomous, ethical" choices about their own health and the health and well-being of their families.[118]

The Power of Narratives in the UAW's Case

The narratives presented by the ACLU brief in support of the UAW depict women unconscionably forced into choosing between surgical sterilization and economic survival:

[Vicky Buttice]: I thought that I would be exempt from the policy because my husband had had a vasectomy. However the plant manager told me that even though my husband had been sterilized, I could still "screw around." I was informed by a personnel representative that I could definitely keep my job in the high lead area if I would agree to being sterilized...I refused...and within a few days, I was laid off. I eventually took a job at a fast-food restaurant at a substantial cut in pay.[119]

Women were subjected to the humiliation of public knowledge of their reproductive status:

["Jane Doe" 6]: The men in the plant knew about the policy and they knew I was sterilized. Some of them harassed me, making jokes and cruel comments...Someone put a can in my locker with the message, "You didn't have to have it done in the hospital, you could have had it done in the maintenance shop." Some of the men referred to me as "one of the guys."[120]

Women were subjected to direct pressure to be sterilized:

["Jane Doe" 8]: When I was sent back to the foundry, I had to have a blood lead test every three months, and at almost every test the nurse suggested that I have a tubal ligation.[121]
[Betty Riggs]: I believe that management pushed sterilization because they made it clear in the meetings that the only form of birth control they considered safe was sterilization. I had asked in one of our meetings whether my husband's vasectomy was adequate protection against my becoming pregnant and was told that it was not. According to the company's representative, I could still fool around and get pregnant. I decided to have the sterilization [at the age of twenty-six] because I needed to keep my job.[122]

Brothers, fathers, and husbands suffered for lack of concern over their health:

[Alva Lewis]: My brother worked in the foundry and the melting area melting ore for about twenty-six years, but as far as I know he had only one blood [lead] test...In 1980 or 1981 he collapsed on the job melting ore [iron] in the melting area. My brother was forty-four years old when he had the heart attack, and due to the events surrounding his heart attack, I strongly believe his heart attack may very well have been caused by the many years he spent working in the high lead melting area.[123]

The UAW also introduced images of the "good mother" and the "bad boss." Who, they ask, should we presume has the greater interest in fetal health? Women's primary incentive for work is to support their families, and so their employment at Johnson Controls is essential, and not antithetical, to family health. The UAW also successfully impugned the intentions of Johnson Controls by suggesting the company was concerned about only those risks to fetal health for which the company might be held liable. During oral testimony before the Supreme Court, a number of the justices drew parallels between the risks of cigarette and alcohol exposure for pregnant women and the risks of lead and questioned Johnson Controls' good intentions:[124]

Justice Scalia: Women in that condition should not smoke cigarettes and drink substantial amounts of alcohol, either, but the Government does not have laws that take the judgment of whether to do it or not away from them. And do you know how this risk [from lead exposure] compares to the risk of harm to the fetus from heavy smoking?

Mr. Jaspan: I don't know the exact comparison, Your Honor, but there's a difference here between the Government prohibiting it and insisting that a—private employer do it. We don't provide cigarettes to our pregnant employees or fertile employees or any other employees.

Justice Scalia: ... What I'm suggesting is that the Government has not shown in other indications an unwillingness to leave the health of the fetus up to the judgment of the mother, including situations where the fetus might be placed at substantial risk, maybe greater risk than would occur from lead poisoning.

Mr. Jaspan: And I—I agree with you on that point. However, we are not dealing with whether the Government puts a restriction on an individual. Here, we're dealing [with] whether an employer, a manufacturer, is required to expose the individual, to expose the child.

Justice Kennedy: Do you take the position that you could refuse to sell cigarettes to pregnant women employees?

Mr. Jaspan: Certainly. I think the employer takes the position that, consistent with its entire health and safety program, that it won't sell cigarettes to *anyone.*

Justice Kennedy: No, but that wasn't my question.

(Laughter)

Mr. Jaspan: Could it single out pregnant employees? ... I assume they could do so, yes ...

Justice Kennedy: I think that's consistent with the theory of your case.

A number of critical points are made in this exchange. First, Johnson Controls admits that it fails to protect women from substances other than lead which clearly pose risks to fetal health, thus throwing the true intentions of the policy into question. Second, Justice Kennedy recognizes that restricting the work of women could lead to more invasive and general restrictions on their behavior. Justice Kennedy points out that allowing Johnson Controls the power to regulate personal behavior under this circumstance may compromise the individual right to "free contract," or individual freedom from state regulation, under other circumstances. From a politically conservative point of view such as Kennedy's, there is a great deal of incentive to strike down this policy.

Most important, though, is Justice Scalia's recognition that it is improper to override the judgment of the pregnant woman with the judgment of bosses or government agents on the question of fetal health. The case was decided on technical legal grounds, but this point more than any other helped make the Court's decision unanimous.

A Feminist Victory

On March 20, 1991, the Supreme Court affirmed the UAW's position in a unanimous decision. The decision affirmed the right of pregnant and fertile women to work and denied the company's claims that it had the right to manage women's decisions about reproduction and work. Justice Harry Blackmun, writing for the Court, asserted that "Concern for a woman's existing or potential offspring historically has been the excuse for denying women equal employment opportunity ... It is no more appropriate for the courts than it is for individual employers to decide whether a woman's reproductive role is more important to herself and her family than her economic role."

The Court refused to affirm fetal protection policies or the traditional assumptions about women, motherhood, and work on which they were based: that only women are responsible for childbearing and childrearing (thus the lack of concern about paternal exposure to toxins); that all women are ready, willing, and able to procreate (thus the exclusion of women as a class from hazardous jobs); that women do not make rational decisions about reproduction (thus the imposition of external controls by government or business); and that women are not an essential part of the workforce and will not be harmed by loss of work (thus the failure to protect women from loss of wages or seniority when excluded from jobs).

A challenge to fetal protection policies, as shown by the arguments in the Johnson Controls case, was also a challenge to those ideological constructs which supported the foundations of women's secondary position in the labor market—the physical and ideological separation of women's roles as workers and mothers.

Judges, legislators, and regulators are subject to competing pressures in an era of complex change in gender relations. These state actors are pulled in one direction by the legal notion of women's right to free contract, and pulled in another by deeply embedded cultural assumptions about the primacy of motherhood and the protection of the fetus. When women's needs as workers have collided with women's needs as mothers, the state has historically come down on the side of motherhood (and a traditional gender division of labor). The Supreme Court decision in Johnson Controls signals a major shift in this pattern.

The decision challenges the traditional dichotomy between family and work concerns, and addresses the ways in which work and motherhood actually intersect and conflict for women. It strikes down fetal protection policies precisely because they force women into unacceptable trade-offs between family and work responsibilities. It questions the requirement that women give up their ability to have and raise children in order to break into the masculine workplace.

The Court was able to reach such a clear decision in the Johnson Controls case because the company's policy was so extreme. It excluded all fertile women regardless of age or marital status, even those whose husbands were infertile. The image of "fertile" women with gray hair and grown children on the steps of the Supreme Court protesting this policy played an important ideological role in this Court decision.

A less restrictive policy—one that excludes only pregnant women, that excludes women from exposure to a toxin whose risk to men is less clear—may still be permissible under the law. The

Court's decision does not preclude the possibility that less restrictive and less controversial policies will be approved in the future. Indeed, as lower courts affirm fetal rights in other areas of law, such as in the regulation of abortion, the likelihood is great that new forms of fetal protectionism will emerge in the workplace again.

What has happened at Johnson Controls and other battery production facilities since the Supreme Court's decision? Some employers have shifted from excluding women to discouraging them from high-risk jobs. Others have kept jobs open to women, but have required that women (and not men) sign waivers absolving the company of responsibility for any reproductive harm caused by lead exposure. Both policies are illegal under health and safety and anti-discrimination laws. One company proposed that all women applicants be required to read the following company warning: "The use of lead in our manufacturing operations creates a lead absorption risk for employees. That risk varies throughout the plant...Scientific and medical evidence indicates that a woman capable of bearing children can cause damage to the brain of her unborn child if she works around lead with lead levels higher than those in her home. The Company strongly recommends that women of childbearing capacity not seek jobs."[125] Other employers have engaged in forms of backlash, refusing to accommodate pregnant women or women trying to conceive (through voluntary transfers to less dangerous work, for instance), arguing that the Johnson Controls decision prohibits them from offering "special treatment" to women. Continuing organization of women workers and vigilance in the courts will be needed to transform the workplace, even with the support of a strong court decision.

The Occupational Safety and Health Administration (OSHA) regulates only three substances (in addition to radiation) for their effects on reproductive health—DBCP (dibromochloropropane), lead, and ethylene oxide—even though at least five hundred substances are known or strongly suspected to damage male and female reproductive health. The OSHA standards still do not adequately address male risks.[126]

As in the case of Angela Carder, success in this case required an alliance between women workers and a predominantly male institution, in this instance the UAW. Perhaps the most significant difference between this struggle over labor protectionism for women and those that occurred at the turn of the century is that previously labor unions had lined up on the side of excluding women from "men's work," but now major labor organizations had lined up on the side of women's inclusion and "gender neutral" work rules. This is arguably because declining industrial labor unions now need the support of women workers. Yet the UAW's success also required shifting their focus away from the specific needs of women and emphasizing the reproductive risks shared by all workers. Nonetheless, their success did shift political debate away from fetal health and toward the health concerns of both men and women.

Sameness, Difference, and Gender Equality

Although it can be seen as a victory for feminist and labor groups, the Johnson Controls decision revealed the limitations of both the "protection" and the "equity" paradigms in current political debates over reproductive health and fetal rights at work. Headlines about the decision indicated the problem of relying exclusively on the standard of equal treatment: "Women Are Now Free to Choose Dangerous Jobs"; "Women Win High-Risk Jobs"; "Court Backs Right of Women to Jobs with Health Risks"; "Women's Right to Risky Jobs Is Affirmed." Women had won the right to enter the male workplace, but at what cost and on whose terms?

The controversy surrounding fetal protection policies touches on political and philosophical questions regarding the very definitions of gender equality and gender difference. Feminists are faced with a paradox: To ignore difference is to risk placing women in a workplace designed by and for men, with all of its hazards and lack of concern for the preservation of health and life. On the other hand, to treat women differently from men in the workplace is to reinforce those assumptions and economic structures which form the foundation of women's inequality.

Neither paradigm adequately addresses the larger risks to reproductive health for both men and women posed by the numerous reproductive toxins workers are exposed to. A political discourse that grants women access to the workplace on the same basis as men fails to address the differences in the effects of exposure to hazardous substances. While the Court struck down assumptions of gender difference in the case of lead exposure, it did not provide a clear direction for cases where women may, in fact, be at higher risk than men—situations where low levels of exposure may seriously affect fetal development but pose a lesser risk to adults. In other words, although gender difference in reproductive toxicity has been exaggerated, it may not be completely dismissed. The gender neutrality model, in such cases, fails to question standards of workplace safety which are inherently "gendered" because they are based upon the assumption that workers never bear children. New definitions of gender equality at work, therefore, must be developed in the context of recognized difference.

In the truly equitable workplace, the conflict between work and parental responsibilities would be transcended for men *and* women. An alternative definition of gender equality that recognizes and incorporates difference would require that *all* of the needs specific to pregnant women were addressed by workplace policies, not just those that pose a liability risk to employers. It would result in policies that reduced toxic exposures for all workers, modified work rules for pregnant women (such as excusing them from lifting or standing), and provided more flexibility for both men and women faced with conflicts between work and family care.

Alternative approaches must also address the politically and morally complex issues of fetal rights. Questions about women's right to privacy and reproductive choice can be addressed only by reasserting the essential, inseparable interest of mother and fetus. Such an understanding squarely challenges the presumption that either the state or the corporation has a greater investment in the protection of fetal health than women have themselves. The fetus is, after all, a part of the pregnant woman's body. Although from a feminist perspective it can be risky to place the right to pregnancy and fetal health at the center of discourse, the risks of excluding these issues are far greater for women.

In the end, an alternative paradigm must address the conflict between health and work faced by all workers, a conflict which can only be resolved through a "life-affirming" ethic. The fact of pregnancy means that women will face this conflict between health and work differently than men. The consequence of denying this aspect of gender difference is to continue to put women in the untenable position of having to choose between their right to have healthy families and their right to economic subsistence. Although construed originally as problems for women only, questions of reproductive health at work may now contribute to new health and safety standards and new relations between family and work for all workers.

4

The Politics of Vengeance:
The Case of Jennifer Johnson

ON JULY 13, 1989, Jennifer Clarise Johnson became the first woman in the United States to be convicted of delivering drugs to a minor by "delivering" cocaine through the umbilical cord to two infants after they had been born, but before the cord had been cut. On October 3, 1987, Jennifer Johnson had given birth to a son, Carl. The obstetrician who delivered the baby reported that the birth was normal and the child appeared to be healthy. Because Johnson had admitted to her pediatrician that she had used cocaine the night before she delivered, a toxicological test was performed shortly after the child's birth on the mother and the baby and both tested positive for benzoylecgonine, a metabolite of cocaine.

In January 1989 Johnson again gave birth, this time to a daughter, Jessica, again with no apparent complications. Johnson had informed her obstetrician that she had used cocaine the morning she went into labor. In fact, she had been hospitalized in December 1988 for a crack overdose and had expressed concern at the time that her overdose might endanger her pregnancy. The obstetrician ordered toxicological tests on both Johnson and her newborn daughter. Again, both tested positive for metabolites of cocaine.

After the birth of her daughter, the hospital reported the birth of a "cocaine baby" to the Florida Department of Health and Rehabilitative Services, which undertook an investigation. Johnson told the investigators that she had smoked crack cocaine or marijuana three to four times every other day throughout her pregnancy and that she had been addicted to cocaine for the past three years. The case worker assigned to investigate the case notified the Seminole County Sheriff's Department of the positive drug tests. Detective

Dan Prast, of the Sheriff's office, then initiated criminal charges against Johnson for delivering drugs to a minor. Johnson pleaded innocent. In 1989 a trial court convicted her of the charges.

Upon her conviction, Johnson was sentenced to fifteen years' probation and one year of drug treatment in a residential program. During those fifteen years, she would be required to report to the court if she became pregnant. She was forbidden from going to bars or restaurants where alcohol was served. She was to be subject to random drug and alcohol testing. And she was required to stay employed or face permanent loss of custody of her children, both of whom had already been taken from her temporarily.

On July 23, 1992, three years after her conviction, the Florida Supreme Court struck down the order of the lower court, arguing on strict statutory grounds that the state law under which Johnson had been convicted had been used inappropriately because it was never intended for the purpose of prosecuting drug-addicted pregnant women. Judge J. Harding, writing for the majority, stated, "The Court declines the State's invitation to walk down a path that the law, public policy, reason and common sense forbid it to tread." Johnson has not yet regained custody of her children, nor has she recovered from her addiction.[1]

THE IMAGE of the pregnant addict is deeply troubling, representing as it does the paradox of a woman simultaneously engaged in the destruction of life (addiction) and the perpetuation of life (pregnancy). There is something terribly disturbing about a woman so deeply torn between the embrace of death and the renewal of life which pregnancy represents. The birth of an addicted baby violates what we think of as an imperative of human society—that we care for and nurture, if not ourselves, then at least our children.

When communities are confronted with events that seem tragic and inexplicable, there is a great need to reestablish some sense of order by identifying a culprit. Assigning blame puts disturbing events back into the realm of human control, reestablishing our sense of security by locating a source of the disruption. Our culture and our laws encourage us, even require us, to fix blame on individuals and to downplay social forces beyond the individual's control.

The push to prosecute drug-addicted pregnant women for drug delivery or "fetal abuse" does not arise solely from conservative attempts to seize control over reproduction and to reinforce patriarchal motherhood. It is also rooted in the social dislocation experienced more generally by men and women when confronted with the pregnant addict. The issues raised by the pregnant addict tap a deep reservoir of ambivalence and uncertainty about the changing nature of men's and women's relationship to motherhood and reproduction. For some, the pregnant addict embodies the social decay and disorder associated with challenges to the nuclear family and traditional gender relations. For others, the prosecution of pregnant women represents the cruelest sort of backlash against those women who are most vulnerable to attack—women whose lives are deeply constrained by poverty, violence, and addiction.

Media presentations of "crack babies" dying of strokes or heart attacks at birth call up our deepest fears of a social order gone terribly wrong. Even the lowest estimates of the number of addicted babies signal a social crisis which calls for our immediate attention and action. But action in which direction? The power of the state to endorse interpretations of cultural symbols is critical in determining where we assign culpability and whom we absolve from blame in this crisis.

The actions of the state, particularly in times of social crisis, can shape the ways in which citizens make sense of new or disruptive social events. Government actions, through the courts, executive agencies, and legislatures, direct public attention toward some social problems and away from others, assign blame or responsibility for those problems, and shape our understanding of what appropriate solutions might be. In more general terms, state actions never just regulate behavior, but act as forms of communication about what is right, proper, natural, or just. State actions legitimatize and institutionalize a particular view of the world and help shape, as well, the self-understanding of citizens.[2]

Judges, legislators, and policy makers are thus "educators" who have the power to articulate (and shape) the concerns of the community.[3] Public policy serves two distinct functions: an *instrumental* function, regulating behavior and enforcing rules, and an *expressive* function, articulating the broader moral and ethical

assumptions of a community. Some public policies are less important as instrumental mechanisms than as expressions of standards
of proper social behavior. As Joseph Gusfield writes of drinking
and driving laws, what the law tells us to *do* is not as important as
what the law tells us to *be*. Legal cases dramatize the moral notions
of the community and, in times of social crisis, literally play out in
public the community's confusion or ambivalence about shared
moral concerns.[4] A consensus in the courts, executive agencies,
and legislatures on a particular policy question confers powerful
authority on the state to shape how we view a social problem and
to assign culpability or blame. When such consensus exists, the
dominant policy approach may appear to be the only one that
"makes sense."

The narratives or stories which are associated with public policies may bear little relationship to the actual social facts related to
a policy problem. Contesting a policy which is driven by public
mythology rather than by empirical fact may require challenging
the myth upon which the policy is based as well as understanding
the social need which the myth fulfills. Judith Hicks Stiehm has
written, in relation to policies excluding women from combat duty
in the military, "When evidence can so easily dispel a policy justification, one begins to understand that one is not really engaged in
disproving but in demythologizing. And demythologizing can be
a futile activity if the underlying need for a myth continues."[5] Current policy regarding pregnancy and addiction serves just such a
mythological function. Challenges to the dominant approach of
criminal prosecution therefore must "demythologize" the concept
of the pregnant addict as well as address the underlying sense of
moral crisis over women's relationship to motherhood.

In this chapter I examine the process by which the myths
regarding the pregnant addict emerged in public discourse and
became encoded in criminal legal cases. I analyze, as well, the
nature of public discourse on pregnancy and addiction, the deep
connections between science, power, and truth underlying this
discourse, and the great need to blame which generated and continues to fuel efforts to prosecute pregnant women for addiction.

These cases raise questions common to all fetal rights cases:
Why do we tolerate some kinds of risk to fetal health (such as lack
of prenatal care or violence against pregnant women) but not

others (such as drug abuse)? Can maternal interests be seen as separable from fetal interests? Does the pregnant woman gain a "duty to care" for the fetus in pregnancy? Does the state have a compelling interest in fetal health, particularly in those cases where a pregnant woman's actions harm both her own health and the health of the fetus? To what extent can the coercive powers of the state enforce that interest?

Fetal rights cases involving drug addiction raise a unique series of problems and paradoxes for feminists. In previous chapters I have suggested that the defense of women's self-sovereignty has rested on two central arguments: first, that women are rational enough to make their own choices about fetal risks (in cases involving forced medical treatment and reproductive risks at work); and second, that women, and not bosses, husbands, doctors, or judges, are in the best position to defend fetal interests—that the interests of the pregnant woman and the fetus are inseparable, as they are "of" the same body. These arguments become problematic when we turn to cases involving prenatal substance abuse.

In no fetal rights cases has it been easier for prosecutors to question both women's rationality and women's intent to protect the fetus than in cases involving drug and alcohol addiction. To assert the woman's rationality may in fact support the case for prosecution, if one argues that addicted women rationally understand (and disregard) the consequences of their actions. And it is difficult to deny the claim that maternal and fetal interests are opposed when women are engaged in systematic self-abuse through alcohol or drug addiction. If the woman and the fetus are truly "of" one body, then actions which harm her health must pose a threat to fetal health as well—they are actions which threaten the pregnant body as a whole.

The attempt to assign causality in these cases raises further questions. How are we to distinguish the actions of the individual from sociohistorical structures that limit and constrain the individual? Indeed, how are we to distinguish between "self" and "other" in the context of the pregnant body? As other fetal rights cases have suggested, the methodological individualism of liberal political philosophy is insufficient for prosecuting or defending these cases.[6]

Criminal cases against pregnant women also reveal the essential ways in which power relations between the sexes are constituted by moral discourse. This discourse is both informed by and in turn informs state actions. When the law functions as public mythology, rather than as an instrumental mechanism for achieving state ends, legal actions take on symbolic meaning.[7] The actual conviction or acquittal of the pregnant addict is in some cases less important than the "truth" that is conveyed by the attempt to prosecute. The prosecution of addicted pregnant women represents a public drama that places "bad" mothers on display for a public confused (or angry) about motherhood. The symbolic meaning of such cases moves beyond the formal powers of the state to affect more general public perceptions of women. It is important to understand both the legal mechanisms involved in such cases and the wider public discourse which frames, informs, and encourages criminal prosecution.

Pregnancy, Addiction, and the Law

On purely instrumental grounds, the policy of criminally prosecuting women who are pregnant and addicted might be judged an empirical failure. Many people argue that it exacerbates the problem by driving addicted women away from health care providers for fear of prosecution and by making women reluctant to report drug or alcohol use to their doctors. Most prosecutions fail to convict or are ruled illegal (or even unconstitutional) by the courts. Most public interest and public health groups, including the American Medical Association, the American Public Health Association, the American Society of Addiction Medicine, the March of Dimes, and even the National Right-to-Life Committee oppose the prosecution of addicted women.[8] Yet the prosecutions continue.

If these cases function more as morality plays than as good public policy, then are they plays staged and directed by a right-wing movement intent on enforcing patriarchal norms of motherhood? Many feminists have made this assertion, with which I generally agree.[9] But it is inadequate to explain the support for such policies among the general public or the deeply vengeful nature of such prosecutions: the narcotics officer involved in the trial of one woman in Michigan stated, "If the mother wants to smoke crack and kill herself, I don't care . . . Let her die, but don't take that poor baby with her."[10]

On what legal ground has prosecution been based? Since 1985 there have been at least 167 documented cases of criminal prosecution of women who used illicit drugs or alcohol during pregnancy.[11] In cases where race has been reported, 76 percent involve women of color. The overwhelming majority of these are African-American, although Latina women and Native American women have also been prosecuted.[12] Where cases have been systematically challenged in the courts, most but not all have been dismissed on statutory grounds. Judges in most cases have ruled that child abuse laws or child neglect laws, originally intended to prosecute fathers (or mothers) for abusive behavior, may not be legally applied to the "relationship" between the pregnant woman and the fetus.

A wide range of legal mechanisms have been used to target drug- or alcohol-dependent pregnant women. Most often women are charged with delivering drugs to a minor through the umbilical cord in the moments after birth, before the cord is cut. Most prosecutors charge women on more than one count, combining, for instance, charges of drug possession, drug delivery, and child abuse or neglect.

Other women have been charged with simple drug possession based on the evidence provided by the newborn's blood at birth. As the *Los Angeles Times* reported, California prosecutors "plan to use 'testimony' from drug babies against their mothers. If illicit drugs are detected in hospital blood tests of newborns, the medical evidence will be used to support substance abuse charges against women."[13] Toxicological testing has also been used in hundreds of additional civil cases as proof of maternal incompetence and grounds for loss of child custody at birth.[14] Such toxicological testing is controversial because it equates what could be a single or occasional instance of drug use by the pregnant woman with parental incompetence. Toxicological tests can also produce both false positives and false negatives. False positives can occur when a woman is exposed to passive marijuana smoke, for instance, or when she has taken a legal drug such as an antihistamine.[15]

Other women have been charged with child abuse or child neglect for their drug or alcohol use. In one case, Dianne Pfannenstiel, a battered pregnant woman who reported to a Wyoming hospital emergency room for treatment for her injuries, was arrested for child abuse when she tested positive for alcohol.[16] Still others have been charged with second-degree assault or child endangerment after giving birth to children born with signs of fetal alcohol syndrome.[17]

Women who have given birth to stillborn babies, or to babies who died shortly after birth, have been charged with manslaughter or criminally negligent homicide.[18] In 1989, Geraldyne Grubbs was convicted in Alaska of criminally negligent homicide when her two-week-old son died, apparently from complications of her drug use during pregnancy (the prosecution argued that the child died from a heart attack caused by prenatal cocaine exposure). She was sentenced to six months in jail and five years' probation.[19] A woman in Mississippi who gave birth to a stillborn girl was indicted on manslaughter charges when an autopsy report found that the death had been due to her use of cocaine.[20] In Massachusetts, Elizabeth Levey was charged with motor vehicle homicide after she miscarried an eight-month pregnancy following an auto accident that resulted from her alleged drunk driving.[21] Women have also been charged with assault with a deadly weapon (cocaine), a crime that could carry a twenty-year sentence.[22]

In addition, pregnant women who appear before the court on more minor charges have in some cases been incarcerated by the state for the duration of their pregnancies when judges suspected that they were drug abusers. In Washington, D.C., Brenda Vaughn was held in jail for four months on a charge of minor theft, which usually results in a sentence of probation. Because she was pregnant and tested positive for cocaine, the judge sentenced her to jail, long enough "to be sure she would not be released until her pregnancy was concluded."[23]

Since 1989 the state of South Carolina alone has brought eighty-seven cases against women and at least forty-three others have been forced to undergo treatment or face criminal charges.[24] One woman in South Carolina was sentenced to three-and-a-half years in prison on child neglect charges and another was sentenced to ten years in prison. A woman in Charleston who tested positive for drugs in her seventh month of pregnancy was put under house arrest for the duration of her pregnancy.[25]

Women convicted on such charges, like Jennifer Johnson, are often subject to the court's "reproductive monitoring," requiring that they report their reproductive status to the court while they are on probation, often for years.[26] One woman convicted of child abuse in California has been ordered by the court to have the sterilant Norplant implanted in her arm as a condition of her sentencing.

In most of these cases, however, prosecution has been unsuccessful. In almost every state where cases have been dismissed or convictions overturned by the courts, legislators have attempted to establish a statutory basis for prosecution.

In 1991 efforts were made in nine states to amend the definition of child neglect to include prenatal drug or alcohol use (Florida, Maryland, Michigan, Montana, North Carolina, Ohio, Oregon, Rhode Island, and South Carolina); in seven states efforts were made to subject drug-dependent women to additional criminal penalties if they took drugs during pregnancy (Massachusetts, Indiana, Ohio, Oregon, New York, Rhode Island, and Texas).[27] In at least five states (Idaho, Illinois, Oregon, Michigan, and Montana) efforts were made to require health care providers to test pregnant women for drug use and to report or commit them to public facilities (such as hospitals or treatment centers) if evidence of use was found.

In Ohio, proposed legislation required women convicted of "fetal abuse" to be temporarily sterilized with Norplant.[28] Rhode Island and North Carolina sought to broaden the definition of child abuse or neglect to include "the unreasonable consumption of alcohol" or illegal drugs, and Rhode Island to expand the definition of manslaughter to include the death of a newborn due to maternal use of drugs or alcohol during pregnancy.[29] Legislation now pending in Oregon not only expands the definition of child abuse to include prenatal exposure to drugs but requires doctors to administer drug tests to pregnant women and newborns under specified circumstances and allows child service agencies to seek an order for the involuntary commitment of pregnant women to public hospitals or treatment facilities.[30] The governor of Idaho introduced a bill which required that drug-dependent pregnant women be civilly committed. The bill was eventually withdrawn because of opposition, but a similar bill was reintroduced in the next legislative session.[31]

So far, the only legislative efforts to succeed have been in Florida, where the definition of child neglect has been amended to include prenatal exposure to drugs, and in Montana, where relatively nonintrusive legislation requires that health care providers inform their pregnant patients of the hazards of cigarette smoking and alcohol and drug use, but protects the confidentiality of the women's medical records.[32]

Despite this limited legislative success, public sentiment seems to favor the prosecution and incarceration of addicted pregnant women.[33] A survey of the general public conducted by the *National Law Journal* reported that more than half of those polled thought a new mother should be criminally charged if her child was born impaired as a result of her substance abuse during pregnancy. Some 41 percent felt that substance-abusing pregnant women should be jailed to prevent them from continuing to abuse drugs or alcohol.[34] If these opinions prevail, legislation allowing prosecution of substance-abusing women will continue to be introduced and, at least in some states, passed into law.

The Case for Prosecution: Crisis, Transgression, Retribution

In a political culture committed to some fundamental notions of self-sovereignty, how are we led to support coercive actions by the state—actions which, even in the context of criminal prosecutions for drug delivery, seem far more vindictive and punitive? The case for prosecution was built on three notions: *crisis, transgression,* and *retribution.* First, it was necessary to generate a sense of crisis about an epidemic of drug use during pregnancy that called for dramatic, immediate, and extreme action. Second, this crisis, the behavior of these women, was represented as a transgression of the most fundamental instincts of motherhood, violating not just society's law but natural law. And third, the transgression was identified as calling not for rehabilitation but for retribution, because the women committing it intended to harm fetal health or were clearly out of control. Pregnant addicts represented not the lost, confused, or misguided mother, but the *anti-mother.* All other possible causes of fetal health problems faded from view as the pregnant addict emerged in public consciousness as the primary cause, and thus the primary target of state action.

As in other fetal rights cases, the politics of science lies at the heart of debates in these cases. Scientific and political battles have erupted over the most fundamental questions, such as simple estimates of the number of women using (or abusing) drugs during pregnancy and the number of babies exposed (or affected) by their mother's drug use, or assessments of the impact of (or harm from) prenatal drug and alcohol use on fetal health. The sense of social and political crisis was dependent upon the science of numbers.

In order to understand the politics involved in scientific debates over prenatal substance abuse, it is necessary to understand the epidemiological methods used to estimate drug use (and in utero drug exposure) during pregnancy. First, there are a variety of ways to screen for drug or alcohol use. Maternal self-reporting and urine testing are the primary methods of assessing drug use during pregnancy. Some hospitals test the urine of the pregnant woman for traces of drugs (with or without the woman's knowl- edge or permission) either at her first prenatal visit or when she enters the hospital for labor and delivery. Some hospitals test new- borns for drugs at birth, particularly if they suspect drug use by the mother. Others simply ask women about their drug or alcohol use during prenatal visits. Hospitals may record suspicion of drug use based on physicians' or nurses' intuition. Others rely on the presence of physical symptoms of an infant's drug dependency at birth to assess prenatal substance abuse.

There are problems with each of these methods of screening.[35] Urine testing reveals only drug use that occurs in the days before testing. Cocaine can be detected in the urine only if it has been used in the last three days. Marijuana can be detected up to ten days afterward. Alcohol metabolizes quickly and can be detected only for a few hours after use. Urine testing cannot accurately record how often a woman used drugs during pregnancy or the amount of drugs she used. Testing is also selective in that hospitals test for particular kinds of drugs, like cocaine, but not for others, like prescription drugs. Finally, as already noted, drug tests are sometimes inaccurate.

The direct blood testing of infants at birth is also not an absolute measure of prenatal drug use. While it can tell us whether an infant was exposed to drugs just prior to delivery, it cannot tell us the extent of the mother's drug use during pregnancy. It also cannot tell us whether or to what extent the infant was actually affected or harmed by that exposure. The most accurate estimates of newborns affected by prenatal drug use have used discharge records from hospitals to count the number of infants born with drug withdrawal symptoms or other clear signs of drug-related health problems. One study analyzed data from the National Hospital Discharge Survey (NHDS), an annual survey which collects information about 200,000 hospital discharges from approximately 400 hospitals in the United States. Based on statistics from the NHDS survey, the study estimated that approximately 41,000 babies were born "drug affected" in 1988.[36]

Not all infants exposed to drugs or alcohol are born with health problems. In fact, in many of the cases where women have been prosecuted for child abuse for use of alcohol or drugs during pregnancy, the prosecution cannot obtain a conviction because it is unable to document any harm to the infant from exposure to drugs. Jennifer Johnson, for instance, was convicted of drug delivery on the basis of positive urine tests (and her own admission to her health care providers that she had used cocaine), but charges of child abuse were dropped because her daughter was born healthy with no apparent effects from her cocaine use.[37] One complication in such cases is that infants who show no signs of harm from drug exposure at birth may develop behavioral problems from drug exposure weeks, months, or years after birth.

The link between exposure and effect depends on when, how often, and how much a fetus was exposed to drugs or alcohol. In addition, two infants exposed to the same level of drugs or alcohol during pregnancy can experience very different effects, depending on individual hereditary factors. Singling out drug use as the decisive causative factor for such effects is highly political, given the uncertain nature of current scientific research. Its role remains the subject of heated scientific (and political) debate.[38]

Maternal self-reporting may provide a more accurate measure of the use of illegal drugs during pregnancy than drug testing.

Even though we might assume that women would underreport their use of illicit drugs, we could safely assume that they wouldn't overreport their use. Self-reporting gives us a base or lower limit for estimates of drug use.

Reliance on the intuition of physicians or nurses for estimates of drug use, although clearly limited, may provide a count of the most obvious cases of drug or alcohol abuse. But perceptions of drug use by health care providers may also be skewed along race and class lines. At one extreme, health care providers may dismiss as "casual" some forms of drug use more common among white middle-class women (abuse of alcohol or prescription drugs), while at the other extreme they may interpret any evidence of the use of drugs like cocaine or marijuana as chronic drug abuse.

Of course, no screening is possible until a woman shows up at a hospital or other health care facility for prenatal care or for labor and delivery. Screening through health care systems excludes those women who are the worst abusers of drugs—those least likely to enter the health care system voluntarily—or women who have the least access to health care services. In this sense, all of these mechanisms may underreport the use of drugs during pregnancy.

One study has extrapolated drug use during pregnancy through analysis of the National Institute on Drug Abuse (NIDA) 1990 Household Survey. Periodically, NIDA interviews individuals about their use of legal and illegal drugs. National estimates on drug use for different ages and populations can be drawn from these figures. By comparing the overall drug use by women of particular age groups with pregnancy rates for those ages, one can estimate drug use during pregnancy. This study found that approximately 4.5 percent of women used cocaine during pregnancy; 17.4 percent used marijuana; and that 73 percent used alcohol.[39] When they combined their study with research from twenty-seven other studies of drug use during pregnancy, the same investigators estimated that 2–3 percent of all newborns may have been exposed in utero to cocaine and 3–12 percent to marijuana each year.[40]

The number of women using drugs during pregnancy must be distinguished from the number of women abusing drugs. And the number of infants exposed to drugs must be distinguished from the number affected by drug exposure. The ideal scientific protocol for measuring drug use during pregnancy would cross-tabulate each of these screening techniques: testing women for drug use during prenatal visits, testing infants for the presence of drugs at birth, asking women about their drug use and asking health care providers about their assessment of that use, and monitoring infants at birth and beyond for the behavioral and neurological effects of drug exposure.

There are other methodological problems with epidemiological studies of prenatal drug use. One is the elimination of sample bias, that is, making sure that the population of women studied is not skewed along lines that would overestimate or underestimate drug use. Another problem is the elimination of confounding variables. When a child is born with health problems, how do we separate out the effects of drugs from the effects of poor nutrition, cigarette smoking, environmental toxicity, or simple heredity? Most women who abuse drugs are multiple drug users. Many also smoke, work in hazardous occupations, or live in areas where they may be exposed to environmental toxins. We may attribute birth defects to drug use that might rightly be traced back to a woman's exposure to mutagenic substances in the environment, like lead paint in her home. Multiple toxic exposures may combine to intensify the harmful effects of any one exposure.

Another confounding variable, one often overlooked, is the mother's reproductive partner. Studies have shown that a man's abuse of drugs and alcohol (or his exposure to toxic substances) may damage his sperm and cause health problems in the children he fathers. A newborn's health problems can appear to be related to the mother's medical history, but in fact be caused by the father's drug or alcohol abuse or his exposure to toxic substances.[41]

The best way to control for confounding variables is to conduct prospective studies that take into account possible exposures of both the mother and father to drugs and environmental toxins, as well as more general factors such as nutrition and health. Most studies of drug use are retrospective; that is, they ask people about past behavior or they analyze hospital records of past cases. Prospective studies, which actually document or monitor current behavior, are more accurate. Because they are more time-consuming and expensive, however, they are rarely done.

The Creation of Crisis

"Everywhere we turn, there seems to be a drug baby."[42] In 1988 the National Association for Perinatal Addiction Research and Education (NAPARE) released the findings of a national study headed by Dr. Ira Chasnoff, surveying drug use by pregnant women in the United States. The survey attempted to assess the extent to which a woman had used cocaine, marijuana, heroin, methadone, amphetamines, or PCP at any point in pregnancy. The survey collected data from a total of thirty-six hospitals representing different geographic areas across the country, including thirty-four public hospitals in urban settings.[43] Each hospital used different methods for assessing drug use by pregnant women. In some hospitals, estimates were based on urine testing at delivery; in others they were based on maternal self-reporting or other screening mechanisms. Overall, the study found that 11 percent of pregnant women had used an illegal drug during pregnancy. Extrapolating from national statistics on the 3.8 million babies born every year in the United States, Dr. Chasnoff and his associates estimated that 375,000 babies every year are exposed to drugs in the womb.

The study, released at a national press conference, received an avalanche of public attention and was represented by its authors, as well as the news media, as documenting an epidemic of drug use by pregnant women in the United States. The *New York Times* explained the survey's figure on estimated drug exposure this way: "more than 1,000 babies born a day are affected by their mothers' substance abuse in pregnancy." The wording transforms the risk of health effects into a certainty and transforms what could have been a single use of drugs by the mother (perhaps before she knew she was pregnant) into substance abuse.

An article in the *Los Angeles Times* represented the findings in this way: "The problem is pervasive. A 1988 survey of thirty-six hospitals across the country concluded that if hospitals conducted drug screens on every woman admitted in labor, at least eleven per cent would turn up positive."[44] The same story reports that the womb has increasingly become a "battleground" and that "as the number of babies born addicted to drugs increases—to an estimated 375,000 nationwide in 1988—so does public concern."

In the *Christian Science Monitor,* Walter F. Connolly, a lawyer for NAPARE, was reported as stating that "there are 375,000 babies born each year with drugs in their systems."[45] Even in its editorial two weeks later opposing the prosecution of drug-addicted pregnant women, the *Monitor* repeats that "more than 300,000 babies are born each year in the United States with traces of illegal drugs in their systems."[46]

A year after the study was released, a front-page *Los Angeles Times* story repeated that "an estimated 375,00 infants [are] tainted by potentially fatal narcotics in the womb each year." [47] The *Wall Street Journal* reported that "currently 11 percent of the babies born in this country show symptoms of their mothers' drug use."[48] And *USA Today* stated that the same number of 375,000 babies a year are "affected by cocaine because their mother used the drug during pregnancy."[49]

These newspaper stories created a sense of crisis of epidemic proportions: as the *New York Times* put it, "a frighteningly high number of babies are being exposed to cocaine or other illegal drugs in the womb" as drug-addicted pregnant women are "producing a new generation of innocent addicts."[50] A subheading declared a "vicious assault on the unborn child." "Because of cocaine's chemical properties," the story asserted, "a byproduct lingers in the system, repeatedly battering the developing child."[51]

The narrative escalated as it was refracted through the cultural and political lens of the news media. The subject of the story shifted from 375,000 babies whose mothers may have used drugs (perhaps only once) during pregnancy, to babies whose health had been damaged by drug use, to babies who actually tested positive for drugs, to babies who showed symptoms of drug use, to babies who were born addicted to drugs, to babies who were addicted not to a variety of drugs but to crack cocaine.

Women who use drugs become drug abusers, infants exposed to drugs become infants addicted, general drug use becomes addiction to crack cocaine. We witness here the birth of both the "pregnant addict" and the "coke baby." A year after the release of the NAPARE study, a front-page story in the *Miami Herald* reported the "epidemic" in this way: "Health officials estimate that 10,000 'coke babies' will be born in Florida this year; nationally the number might reach 375,000."[52] This use of statistics collapses all distinctions between occasional, recreational, and abusive use of a drug, as any woman who uses a drug during pregnancy becomes the "pregnant addict." The language used to describe this abuse (terms such as "battery") often implies the woman's intent to harm the fetus.

Fetal Effects

Alarm at statistics on the occasional use of drugs by pregnant women is warranted only if we assume that a single use of illegal drugs may irreparably harm fetal health. What is the scientific evidence on fetal harm from maternal drug use? What are the effects of drug use on pregnancy and how have these been represented in the press?

In a presentation to the press, Dr. Ira Chasnoff recounted a story about the "recreational" use of cocaine by one suburban couple to illustrate that "even one 'hit' of the drug can inflict damage on a fetus."[53] The couple had used cocaine "from time to time" for years. When the woman became pregnant, she stopped using the drug in her second month of pregnancy and was drug-free until she was near her due date. As an anniversary gift, her husband gave her five grams of cocaine, "prompting her to break her abstinence." As one newspaper story dramatized it: "It might have been a normal pregnancy, if he hadn't almost forgotten his wedding anniversary. But he did, and rather than go to a department store or a gift shop to pick up a last-minute present, the Chicago husband decided to do something really special for his pregnant wife. He bought her five grams of cocaine."[54]

That night she snorted two grams of the coke, then drank alcohol to "quiet the fetus," who had begun to squirm. The next day, after her husband went to work, she snorted another two grams and then went into labor. On the way to the hospital, she snorted the last gram. The baby was born "relatively normal" but with some paralysis on one side; when the doctors investigated they found that the child had suffered a stroke in utero. The child survived but has learning disabilities and continues to suffer some effects from the stroke. The parents remain unconvinced that the stroke was associated with cocaine use.

Dr. Chasnoff goes on to explain that cocaine can dramatically raise fetal blood pressure, increasing the risk of stroke. "It takes only one hit of cocaine to cause a stroke in the baby before or just after birth," Dr. Chasnoff reports.[55] But this is a story of a woman more than once using large enough quantities of cocaine to cause overdose or death in an adult unaccustomed to the drug. How are we to extrapolate from this story the effects that "one hit of cocaine" might have on the long-term health of a fetus?

Another complication is that while some infants may be fatally affected by even moderate cocaine use, others may be virtually unaffected. What can we say with relative certainty about the fetal effects of drug exposure? The most systematic studies to date confirm that cocaine use during pregnancy is associated with lower birthweight and lesser body length and head circumference of newborns. Cocaine has also been linked to structural changes in the brain. Cocaine acts directly on the neurological transmitters in the brain and so can damage early brain development in the fetus. Such damage can lead to an infant who is unable to deal with stimulation or to a child who displays chronic "impulsivity and mood instability."[56]

There are significant methodological questions about almost all studies on the effects of cocaine. Apart from lower birthweight and lesser length and head circumference, no other effects from maternal cocaine use have been well established in studies that adequately control for confounding variables like multiple drug use, poor nutrition, cigarette smoking, or lack of prenatal care. The absence of scientific certainty has not kept the press from reporting dramatic links between cocaine use and fetal health problems.

Exposures to certain environmental toxins produce very particular health problems or diseases. Exposure to asbestos, for instance, causes a very specific form of lung cancer; the appearance of the cancer is itself virtual proof of prior exposure to asbestos. But the health problems that have been associated with prenatal drug exposure have no single cause. Among the symptoms associated with cocaine exposure that one newspaper account listed were low birthweight, small head circumference, increased irritability, tremors, jitteriness, speech problems, violent and unpredictable behavior, stiffness of the legs, inconsolability, awkward or jerky movements, disruption of the startle reflex, eye defects, respiratory problems, sudden infant death syndrome, gastrointestinal problems, diarrhea, poor eating habits, deformities of the kidneys, intestines, and the genital and urinary tracts, seizures, heart attack, and stroke.[57]

Newspapers further dramatized the effects of maternal drug use through personal accounts: the director of the nursery at D.C. General Hospital was quoted as saying, "Never in my medical career have I seen so much suffering as cocaine has brought... [The babies] are calmed with sedatives or swaddled tightly, but their high-pitched cries cut through the nursery like a drill to a tooth. I cannot sit in that room."[58] Another newspaper reported that hospitals in New York had experienced a 3,000 percent increase in the incidence of "drug babies" during the 1980s.[59]

Dramatic claims about long-range effects of drug use were not limited to the press. A Michigan state prosecutor wrote, "Preschool and lower elementary teachers across Michigan are being warned to watch for developmental, neurological and emotional problems in their young students." Even more frightening, "By the end of the 1990s the first 'crack babies' will be entering their teens. It is estimated that by the year 2,000 about 4,000,000 citizens of the United States will have experienced *in utero* exposure to controlled substances."[60]

EVEN if a crisis of these proportions could be established, it would not necessarily warrant or justify prosecution of pregnant drug users. This sense of crisis could have led to expansion of drug treatment programs for pregnant women. Most drug treatment programs do not accept pregnant women because they fear liability if the woman loses the pregnancy as a result of drug treatment.[61] Nonetheless, the sense of crisis was translated into the push for prosecution of women.

Transgression

The decision to prosecute pregnant drug users arose from the idea of these women's transgression from the instinctual norms of motherhood. The public would have to be persuaded that these women sought intentionally to harm fetal health, and therefore that the best solution would be to break the bond of motherhood between the pregnant woman and child rather than rehabilitate the pregnant woman.

A few media stories illustrate the characterization of the pregnant addict in court cases. In 1989, the *Los Angeles Times* reported that a "pregnant prostitute" showed up at the hospital in labor after snorting three to five lines of cocaine. When doctors told her she would have to have a cesarian section in order to save the baby's life, she refused and tried to leave, reportedly saying, "No, I want it to die." Only after she was told that she herself would die if she didn't have the surgery did she agree to it. The child was born with severe health problems and was put into foster care.[62] James Bopp of the National Right-to-Life Committee commented on the case: "When you have knowing and intentional behavior by the pregnant woman which leads to the likelihood of substantial harm to the child, then you have the kind of situation where the state can act."[63] The county prosecutor wanted to charge the mother with attempted homicide, but had no standing in the law to do so.

Newspaper photos show pregnant women smoking crack cocaine, with teddy bears and other children's toys thrown to the floor at their feet. Visual graphics present the pregnant addict as a literal monster, who systematically poisons the fetus in utero. While the crisis is traced to the introduction of crack cocaine into poor communities in the mid-1980s, the growing irresponsibility of women as mothers is seen as necessary for its spread. The crack mother, a "monster mother," produces a "monster baby":[64] One author traces the word "teratogen," the scientific term for a substance which can cross over the placenta to damage fetal development, to its Greek origins: "to make monsters."[65]

The pregnant addict is a metaphor for women's alienation from instinctual motherhood. The image is made more credible by assumptions that motherhood itself is in crisis. All women, not just drug users, are thought to have transgressed the norms of motherhood. This sense of crisis and transgression is a response to technological changes (such as the ability physically to separate the fetus or embryo, even the fertilized egg, from the woman) as well as to a feminist political movement which has argued that women's connection to motherhood is no longer biological and essential, but socially constructed and voluntary. Fetal rights advocates seized upon women's exercise of reproductive choice— and specifically their defense of the right to abortion—as evidence that women can no longer be counted upon to put the interests of the fetus first.

Cases against drug-dependent pregnant women take these arguments to the extreme. The pregnant woman is characterized as inflicting "a lifetime of suffering on her future child, simply in order to satisfy a momentary whim for a quick fix."[66] Even when babies show no sign of harm from their mother's cocaine use, their judgment as mothers is thrown into question. The judge in one such case asserted, "It's the same as if a mother gave a child a pack of razor blades to play with in the crib. The child might drop the blades out of the crib and not get hurt, but the exposure to danger is the same."[67] Because these pregnant women lack either the will or the ability to stop their abuse of their unborn children, they need to be forced to stop by a "powerful motivating force," the force of law.[68]

Retribution

The prosecution and incarceration of drug-addicted pregnant women operates symbolically as retribution for the women's transgressions. Prosecutions hold up for public display women convicted of past abuse of their infants and presumably provide a deterrent to future abuse.

Some fetal rights advocates who support prosecution openly acknowledge the retributive nature of prosecution.[69] They state their case by appealing to commonsense. How could we not hold individual women responsible for the certain destruction of fetal health caused by their abuse of drugs or alcohol? Court cases and social service agencies offer reports of women who abuse cocaine throughout pregnancy and even appear at the hospital in labor, clutching bits of crack cocaine.[70] Surely no one could defend or excuse such behavior.

Fetal rights advocates also call upon social norms and laws regarding child abuse, drawing parallels between such abuse and prenatal drug or alcohol use. Michael Dorris dramatically presents this argument in *The Broken Cord*, which documents Dorris's search for the causes of his adopted Native American son's developmental problems, tracing these ultimately back to his birth mother's alcohol abuse: "If his mother had been locked up, prevented from even one night of drinking, how much more awareness, how many more possibilities might he now have? If she had come after him with a baseball bat after he was born, if she had smashed his skull and caused brain damage, wouldn't she have been constrained from doing it again and again? Was it her prerogative, moral or legal, to deprive him of the means to live a full life? I had no doubt that there were compelling reasons for her weaknesses, for her mistakes, but reason didn't equal right."[71]

While the media coverage of cocaine use during pregnancy has focused primarily on black women, the coverage of prenatal alcohol abuse has focused on Native American women. A great deal of attention was drawn to the issue with the publication of Dorris's book, which dramatized the effects of alcohol on a child "conceived and grown in an ethanol bath," a child who "lives each day in the act of drowning."[72] His son, Adam, experienced the worst effects of fetal alcohol syndrome: growth retardation both before and after birth, facial deformities and other physical abnormalities, and measurable mental deficits.

Dorris's moving testimony to the tragedy of fetal alcohol syndrome quickly jumped to the top of the *New York Times* bestseller list and was hailed as a "big, revolutionary book," a "masculine, nurturant book," about "integrating science and love . . . heart and mind, love and truth."[73] Dorris was cast as the "new man," a single father who had taken on the herculean tasks of single-handedly raising an adopted child while pursuing research, writing, and teaching at Dartmouth College. He was portrayed as a man of Native American descent who had discovered a human tragedy that threatened the very survival of the Native American community.

Dorris and book reviewers alike tie fetal alcohol syndrome (FAS; or fetal alcohol effect, FAE) solely to alcohol abuse by Native American women. One reviewer reported: "The totally preventable cause of FAS and FAE, which may afflict 70,000 babies a year in the United States, has been discovered to be alcohol only in the last twenty years—thousands of years after alcohol began literally shrinking the brains, cleaving the lips and palates, hunching the backs and clubbing the feet of fetuses in the bellies of drinking mothers."[74] The identity of the victims and the culprits was clear: "As Adam had struggled, so many other children around the world struggled: to tie their shoes, to write their names, to remember to wear a coat when it is snowing outside. *All because their mothers drank.*"[75] Adam's fate was sealed before birth by his mother's neglect and abuse: "Adam's first 'home' in his mother's alcohol-saturated womb had effectively wrecked his chances for any kind of life, regardless of who would come along to try to heal and reclaim him after birth."[76]

Determining Responsibility

The desire for retribution, although perhaps understandable, is not the only possible response to the problem of drug and alcohol use by pregnant women. Yet the women are in some sense responsible for their actions. How do we balance the responsibility of individual women with the social and historical factors that have at least partially determined their lives?

To begin with, we need to examine the general preconditions for holding persons responsible for the consequences of their actions. First, we must assume that they are aware of those consequences. We would not prosecute women for taking (or their doctors for prescribing) a drug like thalidomide, which produced horrific birth defects, if those effects were unknown to them. Second, the person to be held responsible must have the capacity to comprehend harmful consequences, to understand the causal relationship between an action and a result. We do not hold children, for instance, or those who are mentally impaired, fully responsible for harm they may inflict upon others unless we are convinced that they have the capacity for rational understanding of their actions. Third, responsibility is dependent upon the notion of individual agency. To be considered wholly responsible a person must have the ability to be an active agent, to initiate and follow through on her actions, rather than having her actions determined by outside forces, like the will of others or structural constraints. We hold people only partially responsible for their actions, for instance, if they are subject to coercion or if they are constrained by historical or social circumstance so that they could act in no other way.

Ultimately, responsibility is tied to the availability of choice. Alternative paths of action must be available and these must be reasonable alternatives. We must be able to identify a time when the individual had other options (however limited) and chose not to take them. Clearly, race, class, and gender inequality limit an individual's access to a full range of options, but they do not negate all choice. The behavior of poor addicted women may be "determined" in the historical sense that they are born into conditions which they did not create and cannot control, and which set strict limits on their lives, but this does not mean that they lose all power to shape their own destinies. In fact, the greatest testament to human agency is the life histories of those women who escape destitution, hopelessness, and addiction, against all social, political, and economic odds.

Further arguments for holding women responsible for drug- or alcohol-related fetal harm come from the feminist movement, which has insisted that women are both rational and intelligent enough to make their own decisions in life. Women are no longer wards of the state, of their husbands or of their fathers. We can presume that even those without direct access to health care have some knowledge of the harmful effects of alcohol abuse. Those who are addicted to alcohol lack the ability to make clear choices about whether or not to drink. Certainly, Adam's mother's choice to drink was not unconstrained. Addiction is fostered by poverty and hopelessness and by the parental abuse and addiction that Adam's mother herself may have been subject to. (This was a woman who actually died of alcohol poisoning shortly after Adam's birth.)[77] But addictive compulsion does not render one immune from responsibility. Although addiction compromises a woman's capacity to make rational decisions, we still hold addicts responsible for the damage caused by their actions.

Even if we were to say that Adam's mother's choices were impossibly constrained, we might still be led to the conclusion that prosecution was the only acceptable policy response, although no longer on the basis of her individual responsibility. If alcohol-addicted women are not capable of understanding the harm that they do (perhaps because of their own heritage of maternal alcohol abuse) or if they are unwilling to stop their self-destructive behavior, then we may argue that they must be compelled by some other social or governmental force to change their behavior.

There appeared to be a very compelling case for holding addicted women responsible for their actions. But the case for responsibility translated into retribution only once one assumed that drug-dependent women were intent on harming fetal health. In this case, they were beyond rehabilitation.

Dorris expressed his great need to blame his son's problems on somebody or something: "I believed in the idea of external cause. If there was a problem, it must necessarily have a source, a reason, an explanation. If Adam's cognitive ability was permanently limited, as every evaluator seemed to agree, I wanted a culprit to accuse, a disease to blame, a named pathology...I wanted answers."[78] Although Dorris recognizes the devastating social and historical conditions which drove Adam's mother to drink, he ultimately lays the blame at her door.

For Dorris, as for many others who support criminal prosecution, the ultimate answer is incarceration, even sterilization, of women who refuse to stop drug or alcohol abuse. While Dorris "recoils" at the thought of "forced sterilization, paternalistic government programs, men making decisions about women's bodies,"[79] the logic of his argument pushes him inevitably to that conclusion. He affirms the view of Jeaneen Grey Eagle, director of Project Recovery on one Native American reservation, who says, "If a woman is pregnant, and if she is going to drink alcohol, then in very simple language, she should be jailed." In cases where women continue to give birth to babies with FAS, she says, "I've gone so far in my thinking [as to consider] forced sterilization for some of these people. I don't think that's out of the question—I think in the future that's going to be a reality."[80]

It is important to note the differences between the treatment of Native American women and that of African-American women in public discourse about addiction. While stories of Native American women almost always set pathologies such as addiction in the historical context of genocide, stories of African-American women rarely, if ever, place their addiction in the historical context of racial slavery and oppression. An example of the former is provided by one reviewer of Dorris's book: "Neither smallpox nor tuberculosis nor any of the other European infectious diseases (for which Indians had no natural immunity), neither military defeat nor the ensuing neo-colonialism and racism has accomplished comparable destruction of the native peoples. It is alcohol that may now be sowing the seeds of the 'final solution' for Native Americans."[81] In this context, culpability begins to shift from the individual to social and historical circumstances.

In contrast, African-American women are often presented in media accounts as individuals whose reproduction is out of control, as women who produce great numbers of children damaged by drug or alcohol abuse, or who give birth and then abandon babies in hospitals. A nurse was quoted as commenting, "The most remarkable and hideous aspect of crack cocaine use seems to be the undermining of the maternal instinct."[82] Mothers are charged with "dumping" babies on the health care system, babies who can run up tabs as high as $250,000.[83]

These news stories are then used by prosecutors bringing charges against drug-addicted pregnant women. A report produced by a Michigan prosecutor who was responsible for some of the earliest prosecutions of drug-addicted women lifted, word for word, an article about drug addiction and pregnancy from the *Wall Street Journal* repeating stories about black women abandoning crack babies in public hospitals and greatly exaggerated figures of the epidemic of crack use by pregnant inner-city women.[84] In addition, the author reports that the Florida Department of Human Resources estimates an annual cost of $40,000 per child to prepare "crack babies" for school.[85] The private degradation of these women is thereby transformed into a public health crisis.

The Arguments against Prosecution

A broad coalition of groups, including public health workers, civil libertarians, and feminist advocates, launched a critique of the myth of the pregnant addict and argued against the prosecution of pregnant women for using drugs or alcohol. These critics refuted all three steps of the argument in favor of such prosecution. First, they claimed that the number of women abusing drugs was dramatically overstated and thus the supposed crisis had been blown out of proportion. Second, critics questioned the representation of women's behavior as a transgression or violation of mothering instincts, attempting to show that women could be drug dependent and still be "good" mothers who cared deeply about the health of their children, even if they were unable to stop their drug abuse. Finally, critics questioned the efficacy and morality of retribution by broadening the assignment of causality. If women were not solely responsible for the health problems of their children at birth, then women alone should not bear the criminal costs.

Deflating the Crisis

The NAPARE study, these critics argued, dramatically overestimated drug abuse by oversampling women who lived in poor urban areas and then generalizing their rates of drug use to all pregnant women. They also pointed to the study's failure to measure the extent of the women's drug use. More accurate measures of the health problem would estimate not only the number of babies exposed to drugs, but the number actually affected by their drug exposure. From a different perspective, the headlines surrounding the NAPARE study might have read, "Eleven percent of pregnant women report occasional drug use during pregnancy; effect on fetus unknown."

The most comprehensive study to date, conducted by the National Institute on Drug Abuse, estimates that approximately 38,000 newborns are affected by their mother's drug use each year—a much lower figure than NAPARE's well-publicized 375,000.[86] Another recent study compiled results from twenty-seven reports published or presented during the 1980s to arrive at an estimate that 2–3 percent of newborns may be exposed to cocaine in utero.[87]

The NIDA study did confirm, though, that the increase in the percentage of newborns affected by drugs between 1979 and 1987 was consistent with "the existence of an epidemic." Although, at 38,000, the total number of infants affected remained relatively small, and the study showed a 300 percent increase in the number of drug-affected babies born between 1979 and 1987, it did note that statistics for later years "firmly suggest that the large average yearly increases in the number of drug-affected newborns seen during the mid-1980s may have abated around 1988."[88] Many analysts suggest that the increases in the mid-eighties resulted from the introduction of crack cocaine into the general population around that time. But the higher numbers might also have come from increased reporting by health care providers—reporting generated by the 1980s' "war on drugs."[89]

Critics of prosecution also question the scientific basis for the presumption that any exposure of a fetus to drugs or alcohol can cause permanent harm to fetal health. It turns out that the children of poorer women may actually experience greater negative effects than middle- and upper-income women from the same maternal drug or alcohol use. One study investigating the connections between alcohol abuse, poor nutrition, and fetal health effects found that women of different socioeconomic classes who consumed at least three drinks per day during their pregnancies experienced dramatically different rates of fetal alcohol syndrome in their newborns.[90] The children of the lower-income women had a 70.9 percent rate of FAS occurrence, while those of upper- and middle-class women had only a 4.5 percent rate. The study controlled for age, smoking, drug abuse, reproductive history, and other medical problems, as well as socioeconomic status and race.

What could have caused this dramatic difference in the consequences of women's alcohol abuse? The primary answer is food. The upper-income women ate regularly and ate a more balanced diet, including more vitamins and minerals. The poorer women frequently skipped meals and ate mostly carbohydrates. All of these women smoked, drank, and abused drugs at the same rate and yet fetal alcohol syndrome among the children of the wealthier women was "relatively rare," while among poorer women it was rampant.[91] In measurements of other aspects of infant health this pattern was repeated. Children of the lower-income women were more than three times as likely to be hyperactive, more than three times as likely to have attention deficit disorders, and four and a half times as likely to be born with congenital malformations.[92] All of the women in this study abused alcohol and most also used other drugs. While all of these women's children experienced a much higher rate of multiple problems at birth than children of non-addicted women, the consequences of alcohol and drug use were far greater for poor women, chiefly because of inadequate nutrition. The policy recommendation that could be drawn from this study would be to feed poor women who are drug dependent, rather than sterilizing or incarcerating them.

But this information was not picked up, repeated, and integrated into media analysis—partly because the assumption that nutrition is more important than drug use is counterintuitive, partly because it disrupts so many other assumptions we hold regarding race, class, and addiction. Joan Bertin, of the ACLU, and Jeanne Stellman, of Columbia University, attribute the exaggeration of negative effects of moderate drinking during pregnancy to the misuse of scientific evidence: "We've become a society drunk not on alcohol but on random 'factlets' wrested from scientific journals before the ink has dried."[93]

Scientific journals help support the presumption that even small amounts of drugs can harm fetal health by disproportionately declining to publish studies which find little or no association between cocaine use and fetal health risks.[94] The news media also exaggerate the risks of moderate alcohol use during pregnancy. One *New York Times* story reported that "even moderate drinking by women in the first month or two of pregnancy, often before they realize they are pregnant, can impair the child's intellectual ability upon reaching school age."[95] Only later in the story do we find out that the study discussed in this article equated moderate drinking with three or more drinks per day. And the evidence of intellectual impairment of children born to these women was simply an average I.Q. score five points below the control group. The director of the study, Dr. Ann Streissguth of the University of Washington School of Medicine, is reported as recommending that women do not drink alcohol at all during their pregnancy: "The effects on children occur even at the social drinking level. The women in our study did not see themselves as having alcohol problems."[96]

At the end of his book Michael Dorris recounts that he asked a pregnant woman not to drink after he saw her order a martini at a restaurant: "There was a part of me that wanted to make a citizen's arrest or to plead for her baby's brain cells." The woman ignored his warnings and finished her drink.[97] In a similar incident, two waiters in a Seattle restaurant refused to serve a drink to a pregnant woman (who happened to be past her due date and who hadn't consumed alcohol during her pregnancy), leaving on her table instead the warning label peeled from a beer bottle. Said one waiter, "I just set it on the table and I said, 'This is just in case you didn't know.'"[98] What is surprising is that they were actually fired for harassment.

Biased science as well as skewed media reports combined to exaggerate the crisis of drug and alcohol abuse among pregnant women.

Refuting the Notion of Transgression

The second point critics of prosecution focus on is the question of addicted women's transgression against motherhood. Pregnant women are depicted as uncaringly persisting in drug or alcohol abuse despite the possible harm it may cause to their fetuses. In fact, most drug- and alcohol-abusing women seek treatment, but treatment is not available. Two-thirds of the major hospitals in fifteen cities in a 1989 survey conducted by the House Select Committee on Children, Youth and Families reported they had no place even to refer drug-dependent pregnant women for treatment.[99]

Thus pregnant women who continue to use drugs cannot be characterized simply as bad mothers. Jennifer Johnson sought treatment for her addiction, her lawyer stated, but could find none in her county. In the state of Florida in 1989, there were reported to be 135 treatment beds available for the more than four thousand pregnant drug-dependent women in the state.[100] The American Civil Liberties Union had to sue four drug and alcohol treatment programs in New York City to obtain equal treatment for pregnant addicts.[101] Most women are so concerned about their use of drugs or alcohol during pregnancy that they volunteer information about it to their physicians. Many of the women prosecuted actually sought out regular prenatal care, despite their continuing to use drugs.

The perception of transgression is directly tied to race and class. We are more ready to perceive poor black women, for instance, as abusive mothers and more ready to excuse the use of prescription drugs or alcohol by middle-class white women. Those who criticize the focus on prosecution also argue that only some women are targeted. One 1990 study of pregnant women in Pinellas County,

Florida, found that although white women and black women were equally likely to use illegal drugs or alcohol during pregnancy, black women were almost ten times as likely to be reported to the authorities for drug use. The study conducted urine tests for the presence of drugs in women at both public and private health facilities at their first prenatal care visit and found that approximately 14–15 percent of all women tested positive for drugs at this first visit regardless of race or class. Yet only 1 percent of the white women were reported to authorities, while over 10 percent of the black women were reported, resulting in some cases in the woman's loss of custody of the child.[102]

How do we compare the care children might get from mothers who deeply love their children but are unable to stop their drug or alcohol abuse with the care their children might receive in an increasingly ineffective state foster care system? How do we compare the destructive effects of a mother's drug dependence with the destructive effects of a father's addiction, when the father may be much more likely to physically abuse his wife and children? Why do we not submit drug-abusing fathers to sterilization, incarceration, social surveillance, and condemnation? Do we punish fathers who are convicted of drug use more severely than we punish men without children, because we can assume that their addiction must have harmed their children in some important way?

Standards for good parenting must be disentangled from gender ideology, which links only women's behavior to the well-being of children. Assumptions about drug and alcohol use must also be disentangled from race and class biases, which implicate only those women who do not conform to standards of behavior viewed as acceptable for the white middle-class. Social responsibilities for fetal health, in the long run, must be shared by both men and women.

The Bankruptcy of Retribution

Critics of prosecution argue that the threat of retribution is an inappropriate and ineffective basis for public policy. Prosecution fails to address the causes of fetal health problems that are outside the control of individual women. For instance, men play an important role in fetal health. In the most direct way, men's chronic drug and alcohol use has been shown to damage sperm and thus adversely affect fetal health.[103] Many women's addictions are deeply tied to their emotional or economic dependence on men—men who may have encouraged or actively promoted their use of drugs, or who may see women's recovery from addiction as a threat.

Prosecution of the woman for drug or alcohol abuse fails to take into account the wide range of factors that can harm fetal health. Infants exposed to drugs in utero typically have lower birth-weights than infants who have not been exposed; one study showed that infants born to women who used cocaine during pregnancy weighed, on average, one pound less than infants born to women who did not use cocaine. But when controlled for other variables such as cigarette smoking, use of other drugs, and poor nutrition, the loss of birthweight attributable to cocaine was only one-quarter of that pound.[104] In fact, according to a number of studies, cigarette smoking is responsible for lowering birthweight by an average of one-half pound.[105] Cigarette smoking has also been well documented as contributing to the likelihood of sponta-neous abortion and sudden infant death, as well as a whole host of health problems later in childhood.[106]

The focus on drug use during pregnancy also fails to account for the damaging effects of other toxic substances, including environ-mental or occupational exposures. It also fails to consider toxic exposures or drug use that could affect reproductive health long before a woman conceives. Women who may be at risk for fetal health problems may not be identified as long as the focus remains on drug use during pregnancy itself.

The point here is not to contest that cocaine use, or any other form of drug or alcohol abuse, is bad for infant health, but rather to illustrate the difficulty of assigning causation of infant health problems to any single factor. Focusing on drug use leads to the perception of the behavior of individual women as the primary cause of the problem, and encourages their prosecution motivated by the desire for retribution.

From Prosecution to Social Empowerment

Alternative policy approaches to the health problems of infants born to women who abuse drugs and alcohol must first address the underlying social forces which contribute to the cycle of addiction. Most pregnant addicted women are also victims of violence and abuse.[107] Some studies have suggested that women's use of drugs or alcohol during pregnancy is an attempt to "self-medicate" in order to relieve the pain of domestic violence.[108]

Most addicted women have little or no access to health care or prenatal care. As a result, poor inner cities experience extremely high rates of infant mortality. Washington, D.C., for instance, has an infant mortality rate triple that of the nation as a whole (32 deaths per 1,000 births).[109] The infant mortality rate in Harlem is more than two times that of New York City as a whole (25 deaths per 1,000 births).[110]

Alternative approaches must make drug and alcohol treatment available and tailor treatment programs to the specific needs of pregnant women. Many alternative treatment programs view pregnancy as a special opportunity for intervention and rehabilitation of women with drug or alcohol addictions. One study has shown that addicted women actually reach out for help more often than addicted men, but they do so through their health care providers rather than through traditional treatment programs. Women are more likely to report their use or abuse of drugs and alcohol to their physicians, to mental health counselors, or to family agencies.[111] To turn these relationships into coercive ones by requiring or even encouraging health care providers to report drug abuse by pregnant women to the legal authorities is to undermine one of the very few avenues women use to get help.

In addition, some have suggested that there are differences in the patterns of addiction between men and women and, therefore, in the definition of successful intervention and treatment. Men's resistance to treatment is often rooted in denial; women's resistance to treatment is often rooted in shame. One study found that women "are more likely to acknowledge that they're in trouble, and often report extreme levels of depression and anxiety as well as low self-esteem."[112] While they may not acknowledge their drug dependence, and while they may also engage in "male" patterns of denial and blaming others, women are more likely to engage in self-blame. Drug addiction during pregnancy must also be understood within the context of a culture which teaches women powerlessness and ineffectiveness. The "learned helplessness" which afflicts even the healthiest of women in this society is doubly compounded by the shame and low self-esteem experienced by the woman who is a drug abuser.

The prosecution of drug-addicted pregnant women can exacerbate the problem by further encouraging a woman's self-blame and the sense that her life is out of her control (which it clearly is once she reaches the court). It can also lead women to make decisions that are even more dangerous to the fetus than their drug use. The fear of criminal prosecution has led some women to have abortions rather than face criminal charges.[113] It has led others to avoid the medical care system entirely.

The empowerment of women who abuse drugs or alcohol must be coupled with the idea of responsibility. While I believe that criminal prosecution is never effective, "principled intervention" may sometimes be.[114] If evidence of a woman's addiction combines with evidence of child neglect or abuse, then state agencies must intervene on behalf of the child after it is born. Active prenatal intervention, in the form of the provision of treatment rather than the threat of punishment, must be the basis of a public policy based on compassion for both the woman and her child.[115]

When we are presented with the dramatic consequences of drug abuse for infants, the mother becomes the first and foremost target. But while we may feel for the baby, we must also feel for the woman who may herself be the victim of the hopelessness and despair wrought by poverty and abuse. A woman can rationally and even desperately want a healthy baby but still be tragically driven by addiction to self-abuse. Although it is easier to see a woman's abuse of drugs as a sign of her intent to harm the fetus, it is more accurate to see it as a sign of her own desperation.

Prosecutions of pregnant drug abusers are driven by the belief that there is a crisis in motherhood—that women, in general, are transgressing the fundamental norms of good mothering. Pregnant addicts are simply the most extreme example of this transgression. The pregnant addict thus exists on the same continuum with all women. Women who have not drifted too far may be rehabilitated, but when women cross the boundary to become the "anti-mother," their transgression must be met with retribution. As the political theorist Charles Taylor reminds us, some offenses "do not just represent damage done to the interests of certain other individuals ... They represent a violation of the order, tearing things out of their place, as it were. And so punishment is not just a matter of making reparation for damage inflicted... The order must be set right."[116] Because the actions of the pregnant addict not only violate the law but disrupt the social order, they call for a kind of symbolic action that punishes the wrongdoer and reestablishes the order of gender relations.

Perhaps the most powerful criticism of the use of prosecution in these cases is this: Prosecution teaches retribution. It can never teach compassion for human life. The prosecution of addicted women does nothing to engender a public culture which will foster a true solution to addiction and abuse.[117] The paradox of prosecution is that it attempts to instill respect for human life (the child's) by a process that undermines respect for the mother's status as a full participant in the democratic community.

The targeting of addicted women as the source of blame does nothing to foster a culture of respect and reciprocity. Our collective security can be regained only by expanding our notion of responsibility. We must place the actions of the woman in the context of a broader community, one which tolerated her abuse by her father or husband, one which tolerated the poverty that bred her self-hatred, one which never valued her as a child, and which never before valued her children. We must place her actions in the context of the socially rooted despair that perpetuates her self-abuse. In the end, our social order can be restored only if we *all* take responsibility for the deeply social causes and consequences of addiction and if we harness the power of the state to support not the politics of vengeance but a culture of compassion.

5

Toward a New Body Politics

WOMEN'S relation to the state remains deeply contradictory. As the fetal rights cases examined in this book demonstrate, although at times the courts and legislatures have been used to affirm masculine control over the female body, at other moments they have clearly stood as women's last, best defense against social coercion. Women's ability to resist efforts to restrict, regulate, or criminalize their behavior has depended on their ability to use the power of the state in their own defense—a state which is clearly divided between its support for fetal rights and its need to affirm women's formal rights to citizenship.

The politics of fetal rights suggests critical questions regarding the significance of pregnancy and fertility for women's standing as citizens in the liberal polity. To what extent must women's reproductive status qualify or undermine women's right to self-determination? Or if women cannot be integrated into the liberal polity on the same grounds as men, to what extent must gender equality require reconstruction of the terms of liberal citizenship itself? What, in the end, is the significance of gender difference for women's relationship to state power? Let me return here to the three dimensions of state power suggested in the Introduction—self-sovereignty, political agency, and moral discourse—to reassess the broader implications of the politics of fetal rights.

Self-Sovereignty and Social Empowerment

The right to self-sovereignty can be defined most fundamentally as the right to control one's body—the right to be "let alone" or to remain beyond the reach of public authorities in questions of bodily integrity. The cases of forced medical treatment illustrate how important it is to secure this fundamental right for women. But the right to self-sovereignty also means the right to be a free decision-maker in one's private life, to have a realm in which one can be self-determining.[1] Yet a retreat into privacy, especially for poor women, can never secure the power of self-determination. The power to be a free decision-maker arises not in isolation, but in *social connection* to a whole web of relationships that can empower women in the context of poverty and domination. Self-sovereignty thus is indivisible from social empowerment.

Just as poverty, for Marx, revealed the "political swindle" of the abstract liberal right to free contract, so pregnancy now reveals the swindle of free reproductive choice.[2] A woman who has the formal right to choice, but no access to economic resources, health care, paid parental leave, or quality day care, does not have the free choice to bear and raise children with dignity. A woman who has the choice to continue her pregnancy, but who may in the process lose her right to control her own medical treatment or to make decisions about where to work and what to eat and drink, does not have access to real choice. Her right to pregnancy is burdened or qualified by her loss of civil liberties.

As the Supreme Court now threatens to overturn Roe v. Wade, even the often false promise of reproductive choice may disappear. The reproductive choice enjoyed by women of privilege may be swept away as these women come to share the struggle for real choice that poor women have always faced. When we look at the race and class patterns in fetal rights cases, we see that women of different races and classes have different relationships to state power. Race and class privilege can "buy" rights to citizenship. A woman of wealth may have the ability to resist forced medical treatment or drug testing by getting medical care through a private physician rather than a public hospital. She may be able to buy services like drug or alcohol treatment through private health care systems, where she may be socially insulated from threats of prosecution.

While the threat of prosecution is not shared equally by women of different races and classes, it is critically important to see that the threat is still shared by all women: no woman is exempt from the threat to self-sovereignty posed by the idea of fetal rights. The successful prosecution of a poor black woman for fetal drug abuse has set legal, political, and social precedents that have been used to prosecute white women of privilege. When a prosecutor in Michigan was confronted with allegations that he was targeting only poor black women addicted to crack, he brought similar charges against Kim Hardy, a white woman lawyer who was addicted to cocaine.[3]

This strategy can have unintended results, however. The cultural, economic, and political power that women of privilege use to resist attempts to prosecute them—or to force them to have surgery, or to keep them out of good-paying jobs—can result in critical precedents for the defense of poor women's rights as well. Kim Hardy, for instance, defended herself successfully in court; the precedent set by her case can now be used to defend women of lesser economic means. Similarly, the appellate court decision in the Angela Carder case, upholding the right of a middle-class white woman to refuse medical treatment, can now be used to defend the rights of poor women or women of color who may continue to be vulnerable to social coercion in the health care system. The disproportionate privilege of some women, rather than hopelessly dividing rich from poor or white women from women of color, can be used to defend the rights of all women.

Although the conditions under which women can be denied their right to citizenship have been more narrowly defined, they have not yet disappeared. Women's right to self-sovereignty continues to remain contingent upon a number of other social and political conditions. The defense of women's self-sovereignty is based on the assumption that women are reasonable and rational social actors. In all three kinds of fetal rights cases—those involving forced medical treatment, workplace restrictions, and drug addiction—women's rationality was thrown into question in order to justify state restrictions on their actions. In only one of these cases, the Jennifer Johnson case involving drug addiction, have such claims succeeded. In both the Angela Carder and the Johnson Controls cases, the courts affirmed women's capacity and right to make their own judgments about the risks to their own health and that of their fetuses. It has become increasingly difficult to maintain that women are not capable of making their own decisions, or of bearing the consequences of those decisions. This is precisely because it is no longer tenable in the law to argue that simply because they are women they are irrational or they lack the intellectual capacity to be responsible for the consequences of their actions.

In a sense, drug-addiction cases confirm this principle. A woman's rationality could not be thrown into question unless some other force compromised her capacity to make rational decisions. It was her addiction, not her womanhood, that affected her ability to make rational decisions. Indeed, the case for prosecution depended upon the argument that women, as reasonable adults and not wards of husbands or fathers, must accept responsibility for the consequences of their actions.

Yet, at a deeper level, definitions of rationality and of what actions a reasonable and rational pregnant woman would take are tied to racial and gender inequality. Women who differ from their medical or legal practitioners in race, ethnicity, religion, or class are less likely to be seen as rational actors in the health care and legal systems. Pregnant women's rationality is also bound to a cultural ethic of selfless motherhood. Pregnant women who are unable to affirm their rationality on these terms—women who refuse to submit to medical procedures in what others judge to be the interest of the fetus—lose their right to self-determination. Women's right to self-sovereignty thus remains tied to an ethic of selfless motherhood which legitimates their secondary standing throughout the rest of the social order.

Women's right to self-sovereignty also remains contingent upon the state's interest in the fetus. Women may have the right to self-sovereignty and bodily integrity, but only when it does not conflict with society's interest in protecting the presumed rights of the fetus. If the fetus is granted rights as a person, then the self-sovereignty of women may be undermined by the dual sovereignty housed within the pregnant body.[4] The assumption that two sets of rights may exist within one body makes women uniquely vulnerable to state intrusion, as the state may be aligned with the fetus against the woman.

This risk of state intrusion is unique to pregnancy and so places women at risk in a way that men are not. Although men are essential to reproduction, their involvement in procreation is qualitatively different because it does not literally compromise their bodies in the way that it does for women. Compared to pregnancy, men's involvement in procreation is fleeting. This essential difference cannot be entirely dismissed as a creation of the right-to-life or fetal rights movements.

Women may have dramatically different experiences of pregnancy: the fetus may be felt to be an intruder, one which literally takes over the body of the woman, or the woman may feel that the fetus is an extension of her will and her body. Indeed, a woman may experience both sensations at different moments in pregnancy. Still, to reduce pregnancy to an individual state is to misrepresent this most fundamental human process, in which one human being literally produces another. This is not to argue that the fetus has interests separable from the woman—indeed, it is to argue just the opposite: that the interests of the fetus and the pregnant woman are *unitary*. When a pregnant woman acts in ways that are damaging to the health of the fetus, she is engaged not in fetal abuse but in self-abuse. Her health and the health of the fetus are inseparable.

In this sense, pregnancy stands as a metaphor for all relations of human dependency. The actions of the pregnant woman clearly have consequences for another potential human being. Just like other relations of human dependency, pregnancy involves certain ethical obligations. We might agree that chronic drug or alcohol abuse by a woman late in pregnancy involves moral questions different from those raised by drug abuse by parents. When parents violate those obligations by being neglectful or abusive, we can remove their children. But unlike parenthood, pregnancy involves the physical unity of the fetus with the female body. Parents may be required to provide a safe and healthy environment for a child, but they are never legally required to give their bodies in their child's interest—to donate organs or bone marrow, for instance— even if the life of the child is at stake. Even though we may find the refusal of a parent to make such a sacrifice reprehensible, we recognize that violating the right to bodily integrity of any citizen undermines a deeper principle, one that is fundamental to any liberal polity. Without this right to self-sovereignty, all other rights fail.

Fetal rights cases represent an attempt to undermine this most fundamental principle for women, as they involve the taking of women's bodies in the service of a higher public interest. To enforce moral obligations in pregnancy is to deny women's claims to citizenship at its deepest level. It is to perpetuate a kind of reproductive slavery which subverts the very moral principles of mutuality which such enforcement sought to defend.

Liberal citizenship redefined to include the pregnant body would thus require the redefinition of the principle of self-sovereignty. Self-sovereignty for women means first of all the right to consensual sex. An expanded political agenda must address women's freedom from rape and domestic violence. The right to self-sovereignty also means the right to voluntary pregnancy. Women must have access to health care, including sex education and contraception. Women must have the unburdened right to abortion, certainly at least until the point of fetal viability. The right to voluntary reproduction also means the right to those services which make it possible to raise children with dignity—prenatal care, quality child care, and adequate parental leave. Only after our social obligations to ensure that women have real reproductive choice are fulfilled can we say that women gain individual moral obligations in pregnancy.

In sexuality, in reproduction, and in work, control over women's bodies is central to the system of gender power relationships. The attempt to grant women self-sovereignty thus threatens this system's deepest foundations. Fetal rights cases—from forced medical treatment to drug abuse cases—represent attempts by the state to assert its control over women's bodies. To settle the issues raised by these cases, either we must define women as a different class of secondary citizens, whose rights to self-sovereignty are qualified by pregnancy (or even fertility), or we must demasculinize our notion of citizenship to account for the particular needs, interests, and concerns of women. In doing so, we can challenge the foundations of gender inequality and initiate a new kind of polity for all citizens, one which affirms the rights of individuals to autonomy through social empowerment.[5]

The Pregnant Body and Political Agency

The pregnant body in public is a troublesome thing. It disrupts public structures at a most fundamental level by exposing the essential masculinity of both politics and work. In the twentieth century, women have gained entrance to the public spheres of work and politics only by leaving behind that which made them different from men. Definitions of the good citizen and the good worker are deeply gendered. The "demasculinization" of the public world and the full and equal integration of women into that world thus require a fundamental transformation of the terms of work and politics.

The pregnant woman stands in stark contrast to traditional definitions of citizenship. Whereas the good citizen is rational and transcends bodily necessity, the pregnant woman personifies bodily need. Whereas the good citizen enters politics to defend individual self-interest, the pregnant woman represents the interdependence of human life and the difficulty, even impossibility, of distinguishing self from other. Whereas the good citizen is a patriot and a soldier willing to sacrifice his life for the nation, the pregnant woman symbolizes the preservation and defense of life.

A basic antithesis has existed between pregnancy and politics. Women have been required to deny their connection to reproduction and caregiving in order to be integrated into the masculine world of politics. A public life so defined produces a politics which devalues childrearing and reproduction, attempts to ignore that human beings are born, get sick, and die, and ultimately has produced a militaristic politics which privileges death over life, production over reproduction, instrumental technology over natural processes, and the individual over the community.[6] It is a sad irony of cases involving the criminal prosecution of pregnant addicts that they are at the same moment both the product and the target of a society bent on privileging self-interested consumption over social empowerment.

The pregnant body is trouble in the workplace as well. The pregnant body doesn't punch a time clock and doesn't listen to the directives of bosses. It sometimes has needs for sleep or food that resist the "logic" of shop-floor or bureaucratic discipline. The pregnant body is unpredictable; it disrupts industrial order. It represents life over profits, health over production.[7] Once the pregnant body produces children, the "trouble" is multiplied, as women (and men who care) are torn between the spontaneity and human needs of children and the discipline and rigidity of work.

Just as women have had to deny, suppress, or disguise their needs as women to be integrated into politics, so too women have had to deny, disguise, or suppress their needs as caregivers to be integrated into work. In some cases women literally have to give up their ability to become pregnant in order to gain access to "men's" jobs. But once the trade-off for women between production and reproduction becomes explicit, it also becomes intolerable. What was true for the women at Johnson Controls is just as true for all women (and men) who care for families and children. The pregnant body reveals the essential masculinity of the workplace, a workplace which demands that we subordinate the giving of care and the production of life to the production of profits. The integration of women into work thus demands the transformation of the priorities of production.

Furthermore, what is true for the pregnant body is true for all bodies. Bodies get sick and need healing. Bodies can't always conform to work rules and they don't always bend to the needs of production. If work is not healthy for the pregnant body, that is only because work is not healthy for anyone. The antithetical relationship between pregnancy and work is just one expression of a division between work and bodily need for all human beings. Although work can be the most fulfilling of human functions, most workplaces, driven by the relentless pursuit of profits, subject workers to an inhumane pace of work that deadens the brain and that poisons the body. This is most true for those at the bottom of the economic scale, who may actually die because health and safety protections are politically inexpedient.

Those workers caught most sharply in the conflict between bodily need and production may be most likely to articulate opposition to the cultural and economic machinery which drives relentless production. Because of women's historical role in producing and preserving human beings, it was working women who experienced this conflict between work and family health most acutely and working women who first expressed resistance.

The degendering of the public structures of work and politics requires the redefinition of the public agenda to address the needs and concerns of women. But the fetal rights cases examined here point to a number of paradoxes and risks in this process—that the articulation of "women's needs" will reinforce gender segregation and domination, or that the public articulation of "private" needs will lead to new, more insidious forms of social coercion and control.

As the Johnson Controls case so well illustrates, feminists are now confronted with two seemingly contradictory imperatives. One is that men must be drawn into reproduction and that the differences between men and women be diminished. But the other is that men's power over reproduction must be limited and women's unique relationship to procreation be recognized and affirmed. Women's specific relationship to procreation mandates that women's control over reproduction remain explicit and unassailable. To the extent that women's commonalities with men can be established, political issues can be "degendered"—cast not as a problem for women, but as a more general social concern. To the extent that irreducible difference exists, women's particular social and biological standpoint must be affirmed.

Degendering politics requires drawing men into reproduction. The fetal rights cases examined here suggest the importance of emphasizing men's connection to and responsibility for the reproduction and preservation of human life. This includes recognizing the essential connection between male reproductive health and fetal health. Both the Johnson Controls case and the Jennifer Johnson case suggested that men's exposure to reproductive toxins (either in the workplace or through drug and alcohol use) can contribute to fetal health problems. This development was of critical political importance as it shifted responsibility, and thus culpability, for fetal health problems away from women alone and toward both individual men and larger social forces.

In all fetal rights cases, women have gained the ability to use state power by diminishing assumptions of gender difference, degendering policy issues, and establishing alliances with powerful male organizations—drawing out the commonalities between men and women to reveal the deeper sources of social problems that underlie gender conflict. In the Angela Carder case, degendering involved casting the issue as one of patient's rights rather than fetal rights. In the Johnson Controls case, degendering involved drawing men into the discussion of the sources of fetal health problems and casting reproductive hazards in the context of the general disregard for human health in the workplace. In the

Jennifer Johnson case, it meant shifting the discourse to focus on patterns of addiction common to both men and women. Men who perceived that they too might be jeopardized by policies which threatened women were more likely to use their privilege to women's advantage.

This degendering of the issues also breeds its own potential dilemmas. Pregnancy is clearly a social matter, one deeply affected by a woman's relationship with a man and by the social conditions in which they both live. The womb is not a sanctuary, but is profoundly influenced by environmental conditions and social relationships outside the woman's body. The recognition that pregnancy and reproduction are social processes, and processes which men are essential to, strengthened arguments for men's increasing interest in reproduction. This interest could lead, however, to new forms of repression, in which women could become the objects of increasing social regulation. Male claims to defend fetal health might be affirmed by diminishing the difference between men and women in reproduction.

The feminist movement has historically challenged assumptions of gender difference. Some have argued that gender equality must be equated with the elimination of gender distinctions in policy and the law—that these distinctions always serve to institutionalize gender domination.[8] But all efforts to erase gender categories will ultimately run up against the pregnant body itself, which creates a special set of needs for women.

There are two senses in which gender difference must be affirmed in order to achieve gender equality. First, the particular needs of pregnant women cannot be adequately addressed through gender neutral policy or law. In the fetal rights cases I have analyzed here, pregnant women have needs as patients, as workers, and as drug- or alcohol-involved women which are unique. Though the pregnant patient shares much in common with other patients, and though her right to control her medical treatment must remain absolute, the condition of pregnancy presents certain questions of health and ethics never faced in the same way by patients who are not pregnant. While many of the needs of pregnant workers could be addressed by better health and safety standards for all workers, such standards cannot address all the needs of pregnant women at work. There may, in fact, be times when pregnant women are at risk in a way that other workers are not—for instance, in cases where pregnant women are exposed to high temperatures or required to perform heavy lifting.[9] Protective equipment such as face masks that restrict a woman's intake of oxygen, or protective coveralls, may be ill-suited for pregnancy. Not all pregnant women have special needs in pregnancy and not all occupations pose special risks for pregnant women. But we cannot say that the workplace has been demasculinized until we have looked at work rules and structures from the point of view of the pregnant body and eliminated the physical and ideological barriers that exist for pregnant women.

Fetal rights cases involving addiction point to the need to recognize gender difference, as well. Although adequate drug and alcohol treatment programs could provide far better opportunities for recovery for addicted women, there are unique moral questions raised by pregnancy and addiction. For this reason, pregnancy can be seen as a special opportunity for non-coercive intervention for addicted women. Drug and alcohol treatment must also bear in mind that treatment may present risks for pregnant women that it does not for other addicts.

Gender equality requires the transformation of public structures of power to narrowly and specifically address the needs of pregnant women. This is far different from treating all women as if they were always pregnant or about to become pregnant. Rather, this transformation would ensure that women have the right to be pregnant without having to sacrifice their rights as workers or citizens. It would "demasculinize" public structures in a way that can challenge the embedded masculine antithesis between reproduction and production, between motherhood and citizenship.

The second sense in which gender difference must be affirmed in order to achieve gender equality is that the needs, interests, and concerns of women as caregivers must be reflected in the public agenda. The experiences of women in American history have differed dramatically by race, ethnicity, sexual preference, religion, and class. But in the contemporary context, women are overwhelmingly those who care for the sick, the young, and the old, who see to the daily bodily needs of their fellow human beings. The social and historical standpoint of women as caregivers must be used to define a new kind of public agenda for all citizens—one which affirms human needs over industrial production and profit. Drawing men into caregiving work must also be an essential part of this process.

Women activists have historically used their association with motherhood and their position within the family to raise important social issues.[10] Particularly in times of social crisis, appeals to maternalism have been used to expand the political agenda, not just for women, but for all citizens. Women activists played a crucial role in the early establishment of welfare state programs, extending the "private" values of care and nurturance into the public realm of politics.[11]

Women at the turn of the twentieth century also used their association with motherhood to promote progressive labor policies. Alice Kessler-Harris has shown that appeals to the particular needs of women, especially mothers, were used to affirm the minimum wage for women. Women's special position as mothers (whether real or assumed) could be used by progressive forces to initiate transformative change that otherwise would have been rendered ineffective by conservative ideology. Attention to gender difference thus kept alive the possibility that all workers deserved protection.[12]

Gendered discourse holds transformative potential only if it leads to a restructuring of capitalist or gender power relations. The Johnson Controls case represents a moment in history when a policy paradigm shifted from gendered to degendered discourse. Initial concerns about reproductive health were raised by women, specifically about pregnant women's susceptibility to harm from toxins. Women's concern for reproductive health at work challenged the historical division between production and reproduction, between work and health, violating a basic precept of the industrial workplace. The first response of the employers (and the state) was to reinstate the division between productive and reproductive labor by excluding women and their concerns from the workplace. But the need for women's labor in a changing labor market and political forces which demanded gender equality at work made the exclusionary rules impossible to sustain. The concern for women's needs was ultimately used to challenge the antithesis between work and health for all workers.

Taken together, the fetal rights cases examined here are not so much about reproductive health as they are about reproductive power. Fetal rights cases represent an attempt to establish the boundaries within which women reproduce and to encode these boundaries in law. So far, most of these attempts have been unsuccessful, as the courts have ultimately ruled in women's favor. The three cases analyzed here signal major victories for women in the politics of fetal rights. The Angela Carder case upheld the rights of pregnant women to control their medical treatment. The policy of Johnson Controls was unanimously struck down by the Supreme Court. And the conviction of Jennifer Johnson was overturned.

Yet it is important to be aware of the tenuous nature of the courts' decisions in each case. How might the decision in the Angela Carder case have changed if her child had survived—or if she, like so many other pregnant women who have been forced to undergo surgery, had been perceived by hospital or court authorities as a bad or misinformed or irrational mother? In the case of Johnson Controls, the Supreme Court's decision might have been different if the company's policy had not been so sweepingly over-inclusive or if the toxic substance had not been a known hazard to men as well as to women. And the Jennifer Johnson case, like almost all fetal drug-abuse convictions overturned by the courts to date, was reversed on strictly technical grounds. The public sentiment which drives these prosecutions will surely generate more enforceable fetal abuse statutes in the future.

Moral Discourse and Gender Power

In the face of fundamental changes in men's and women's relationship to reproduction, public sentiment has made women, especially poor women, the "dumping ground" for collective anxieties about social transformation. Pregnant women, in particular, have become the targets of that anxiety as the public repeats the "collective chant" of America's worst fears—fears of broken homes, of addiction, poverty, and disease, of single mothers, of women refusing to give birth, or of women refusing to care for their babies or even murdering their own children.[13] Legal cases act as social catharsis for those most distressed by profound shifts in reproductive power relations.

Women have successfully defended themselves from the threat of legal prosecution only by presenting themselves in public discourse as women whose commitment to motherhood is unquestioned. At this deeper level, the imperatives of gender inequality continue to inform collective moral discourse. Despite their efforts to degender the issue of workplace hazards, the success of women workers in the Johnson Controls case depended on the perception of them as working mothers who sought to support their children and families through work. Public discussion of Angela Carder's case cast her not as a pregnant woman defying the orders of her physician, but as a woman willing to suffer great risks and hardships in order to become a mother.

Such claims for good motherhood have been unsuccessful in public discourse surrounding drug and alcohol addiction. Addiction is obviously antithetical to the health of women and their children. But there are deeper reasons why claims to good motherhood have failed in the drug addiction cases. On a symbolic level, these women represent the "anti-mother"—women who justly deserve the vengeance of the community. Characterizations of the "anti-mother" are deeply racial. The targeting particularly of African American women has helped to perpetuate a politics of retribution.

As long as this characterization remains unchallenged, public sentiment will continue to challenge, and possibly negate, the power of law. Although women's rights may be upheld in the courts, pregnant women themselves will ultimately lose if they continue to be publicly persecuted by a society that considers them irrational, irresponsible, or out of control. A deep reservoir of public sentiment continues to fuel the belief, not only among traditional conservatives but among the public at large, that women are not to be trusted either as mothers or as pregnant women. Until this belief is directly challenged, fetal rights cases will continue to be regenerated in new form.

The virtual invisibility and enforced silence of drug-dependent women in stories of "fetal abuse" have effectively undercut attempts to shift the discourse toward one that affirms their rights. Few media reports actually interview women brought up on criminal charges, leaving the public to project images of the "pregnant addict" or "bad motherhood" onto these women. The content of moral discourse will be determined not by the technical precedents of legal right, but by the symbols, images, and narratives used to talk about the women involved in these cases. For this reason, it is critically important that women be empowered to give voice to their experience, in order to shape moral discourse from their point of view. The experiences of women at the bottom of structures of gender domination must form the basis for an alternative critical discourse on morality and politics.

There is indeed a crisis of reproduction, but it is not a crisis of motherhood. It is a crisis of gender power relations. Women are demanding control over their bodies and over when, where, and whether they will reproduce. Women are refusing to conform to the dictates of gender domination—by entering the male workplace, by resisting the orders of bosses and physicians, and by demanding an equal place with men in the public world. This challenge to gender power relations has produced a backlash in the form of attempts to enforce (or prohibit) motherhood for women.

In the face of this threat to gender power relations, domination of women may be reinstated, but only at a cost. For as tacit respect for masculine authority decays, more coercive and naked forms of power will emerge to take its place. Contests over fetal rights, as an expression of masculine power, ultimately make gender domination explicit and thus vulnerable to change.

GENDER domination takes two forms: one secured by violence and threat, the other secured by morality and belief. At the heart of fetal rights politics, we find both forms of domination bound together. The most stable forms of domination are those secured not by threats, but by gifts. Fetal protectionism is offered as the gift of something that women dearly want—the preservation and defense of fetal health. It is presented as a heroic attempt to save the fetus through remarkable medical technology, to shield the fetus from the inhumanity and toxicity of the industrial workplace, or to rescue the fetus from the tragic consequences of addiction.

In the absence of better alternatives, the gift is tempting. For women in desperate need of medical care, or of health and safety protection at work, or of drug or alcohol treatment, any offer of services appears to be better than none. But bound together with the gift is a threat—the threat of prosecution for refusing to follow doctor's orders, for daring to cross the lines of workplace segregation, for failing to conform to traditional notions of motherhood or the subordination of self in gender power relations. Gifts of the powerful never come without a cost. In the end, the cost—the loss of full citizenship for women—is simply too high to pay.

Notes · Acknowledgments · Index

Notes

Introduction

1. Lynn Paltrow, "Criminal Prosecutions against Pregnant Women: National Update and Overview," Reproductive Freedom Project (New York: American Civil Liberties Union, 1992).
2. Veronica E. B. Kolder, Janet Gallagher, and Michael Parsons, "Court-Ordered Obstetrical Interventions," *New England Journal of Medicine* 316:19 (1987), pp. 1192–96; p. 1193.
3. Cynthia R. Daniels, Maureen Paul, and Robert Rosofsky, "Health, Equity, and Reproductive Risks in the Workplace," *Journal of Public Health Policy* (Winter 1990), pp. 449–462.
4. Brennan v. Smith 157 A.2d 497 (1960) first articulated this right in the law.
5. Muller v. Oregon 208 U.S. 412 (1908).
6. For example, see Jeffrey Parness, "Crimes against the Unborn: Protecting and Respecting the Potentiality of Human Life," *Harvard Journal on Legislation* 22:97 (1985), pp. 97–172.
7. One could argue that the taking of the pregnant body in the service of the protection of fetal health is comparable to male conscription. I deal with this question in the final section of Chapter 2.
8. For an interesting discussion of the disproportionate power of men and women as "publicly articulate agents" see Celeste Condit, *Decoding Abortion Rhetoric* (Urbana: University of Illinois Press, 1990). On the distinction between public and private in gender politics see Wendy Brown, *Manhood and Politics* (Savage, Md.: Rowman and Littlefield, 1988); Carole Pateman, *The Sexual Contract* (Berkeley: University of California Press, 1988); and Jean Elshtain, *Public Man/Private Woman* (Princeton, N.J.: Princeton University Press, 1981).
9. For general discussion on women and public policy, see J. Gelb and M. L. Paley, *Women and Public Policies* (Princeton, N.J.: Princeton University Press, 1987), and Ellen Boneparth, ed., *Women, Power, and Policy* (New York: Pergamon Press, 1982). For specific discussions of the meaning of gender difference for policy and law, see the interesting collection of articles in Deborah Rhode, ed., *Theoretical Perspectives on Sexual Difference*

(New Haven, Conn.: Yale University Press, 1990); Zillah Eisenstein, *The Female Body and the Law* (Berkeley: University of California Press, 1989); and Catherine MacKinnon, *Toward a Feminist Theory of the State* (Cambridge, Mass.: Harvard University Press, 1989).

10. In the words of Peter Corrigan and Derek Sayer, "Out of the vast range of human social capacities—possible ways in which social life could be lived—state activities more or less forcibly 'encourage' some whilst suppressing, marginalizing, eroding, and undermining others." Peter Corrigan and Derek Sayer, *The Great Arch—English State Formation as Cultural Revolution* (London: Basil Blackwell, 1985), p. 4.

11. As Jane Jensen has characterized it, "The terrain on which actors struggle for representation is the *universe of political discourse*—a space in which socially-constructed identities emerge in discursive struggle. As actors with a variety of collective identities co-exist in the universe of political discourse, their practices and meaning systems jostle with each other for social attention and legitimacy." Jane Jensen, "Paradigms and Political Discourse: Protective Legislation in France and the United States before 1914," *Canadian Journal of Political Science* (June 1989), pp. 235–258, p. 238. See also Nancy Fraser on this point, particularly in relationship to welfare policy, in *Unruly Practices: Power, Discourse and Gender in Contemporary Social Theory* (Minneapolis: University of Minnesota Press, 1989).

1. Fetal Animation

1. For excellent reviews of characterizations of the fetus in a variety of historical and cultural contexts see Deborah L. Rhode, *Justice and Gender* (Cambridge: Harvard University Press, 1989); Kristin Luker, *Abortion and the Politics of Motherhood* (Berkeley: University of California Press, 1984); Rosalind Pollack Petchesky, *Abortion and Woman's Choice* (Boston: Northeastern University Press, 1984); and Laurence H. Tribe, *Abortion: The Clash of Absolutes* (New York: Norton, 1990).

2. See Simone de Beauvoir, *The Second Sex* (New York: Vintage Books, 1974) and Shulamith Firestone, *The Dialectic of Sex* (New York: William Morrow, 1970).

3. For historical and cross-cultural analysis of the regulation of abortion see Petchesky, *Abortion and Woman's Choice* and Tribe, *Abortion: The Clash of Absolutes*.

4. Dietrich v. Northampton, 138 Mass. (1884).

5. *In re* Peabody, 5 N.Y.2d 546, 158 N.E.2d 844, 186 N.Y.S.2d 269 (1959). For a conservative perspective on fetal personhood, see John Myers, "Abuse and Neglect of the Unborn: Can the State Intervene?" *Duquesne Law Review* 23:1 (1984), pp. 1–76.

6. For a comprehensive history, see Dawn Johnsen, "The Creation of Fetal Rights: Conflicts with Women's Constitutional Rights to Liberty, Privacy, and Equal Protection," *Yale Law Journal* 95 (1986), pp. 599–625.

7. Bonbrest v. Kotz, 65 F.Supp. 138 (1946).

8. Brennan v. Smith, 157 A.2d 497 (1960).
9. For example, see Jeffrey Parness, "Crimes against the Unborn: Protecting and Respecting the Potentiality of Human Life," *Harvard Journal on Legislation* 22:97 (1985), pp. 97–172.
10. Brennan v. Smith, 157 A.2d 497 (1960).
11. Johnsen, "The Creation of Fetal Rights," p. 602.
12. Parness, "Crimes against the Unborn," p. 140.
13. Ibid., p. 135.
14. People v. Guthrie, 97 Michigan App. 226, 232, 293 N.W.2d 775, 778 (1980), quoted in Parness, "Crimes against the Unborn," p. 131.
15. Ibid., p. 131.
16. Ibid., p. 133.
17. Commonwealth v. Cass, 467 N.E.2d (1984).
18. These states include California, Illinois, Iowa, Michigan, Mississippi, New Hampshire, Oklahoma, Utah, Washington, and Wisconsin. For specific penal codes see Johnsen, "The Creation of Fetal Rights," p. 602, n. 14.
19. See Parness, "Crimes against the Unborn," and Johnsen, "The Creation of Fetal Rights," for details of such laws.
20. Johnsen, "The Creation of Fetal Rights," p. 603.
21. Dawn Johnsen, "From Driving to Drugs: Governmental Regulation of Pregnant Women's Lives after Webster," *University of Pennsylvania Law Review* 138 (1989), p. 179.
22. Emily Martin, *The Woman in the Body* (Boston: Beacon Press, 1987), p. 20.
23. An excellent example is Lennart Nilsson, *A Child Is Born* (New York: Delacorte Press/Seymour Lawrence, 1976).
24. Rosalind Petchesky, "Fetal Images: The Power of Visual Culture in the Politics of Reproduction," *Reproductive Technologies: Gender, Motherhood, and Medicine,* Michelle Stanworth, ed. (University of Minnesota Press, 1987), p. 65.
25. Roe v. Wade at 160.
26. Lynn M. Paltrow, "A Review of Advances in Reproductive and Neonatal Technology as They Relate to Abortion Rights," *Reproductive Rights Law Reporter* (October 30, 1986), p. 24.
27. On fetal viability, see J. Whitridge Williams, *Williams Textbook of Obstetrics,* 18th edition, F. Gary Cunningham, Paul C. MacDonald, and Norman F. Gant, eds. (Norwalk, Conn.: Appleton & Lange, 1989). Dr. Avery is quoted in Gina Kolata, "Survival of the Fetus," *New York Times,* April 18, 1989, p. 15.
28. Quoted by J. Mann, "Fabricating," *Washington Post,* September, 17, 1982.
29. Akron Center for Reproductive Health v. City of Akron 462 U.S. 416, 442 (1983).
30. Bernard Nathanson, *The Abortion Papers* (New York: Frederick Fell Publishers, 1983), p. 2.
31. For an interesting conservative perspective on fetal technologies see John A. Robertson, "Procreative Liberty and the Control of Conception, Pregnancy, and Childbirth," *Virginia Law Review* 69 (1983), pp. 405–464.

32. For information on fetal surgery and other medical treatments see A. Kurjak, ed., *The Fetus as Patient* (New York: Excerpta Medical/Elsevier Science Publishing Company, 1985). Also see Ruth Hubbard, "Legal and Policy Implications of Recent Advances in Prenatal Diagnosis and Fetal Therapy," *Women's Rights Law Reporter* 7:3 (1982), pp. 201–208.

33. Nathanson, *The Abortion Papers*, p. 132.

34. Ibid., p. 134.

35. Quoted in Celeste Condit, *Decoding Abortion Rhetoric* (Urbana: University of Illinois Press, 1990), p. 88.

36. Ibid., p. 86.

37. Ibid., pp. 88–89.

38. All references are to language used in the anti-abortion film *The Silent Scream*, produced and directed by Jack Duane Dabner (Anaheim, Calif.: American Portrait Films, 1984).

39. Nathanson, *The Abortion Papers*, p. 139.

40. Barbara Katz Rothman, *The Tentative Pregnancy* (New York: Viking Press, 1986).

41. Nathanson, *The Abortion Papers*, pp. 151–153.

42. Caroline Whitbeck characterizes this as the "flowerpot" theory of pregnancy, where women are the "pots" and men provide the "seeds." Quoted in Barbara Katz Rothman, *Recreating Motherhood* (New York: Norton, 1989), p. 248, n. 3.

43. Roe v. Wade, 410 U.S. (1973) 162, as quoted in Parness, "Crimes against the Unborn," p. 102.

44. Sam S. Balisy, "Maternal Substance Abuse: The Need to Provide Legal Protection for the Fetus," *Southern California Law Review* 60 (1987), p. 1221.

45. Ibid., p. 1219.

46. Planned Parenthood v. Casey, 112 S.Ct. 2791 (1992), at 2816.

47. Planned Parenthood v. Casey, at 2817.

48. Robertson, "Procreative Liberty," p. 463.

49. Ibid., p. 437 (citations omitted).

50. As Robertson characterizes it, "These obligations may require her to avoid work, recreation, and medical care choices that are hazardous to the fetus. They also obligate her to preserve her health for the fetus' sake or even allow established therapies to be performed on an affected fetus. Finally, they require that she undergo prenatal screening where there is reason to believe that this screening may identify congenital defects correctable with available therapies" (ibid., p. 445).

51. These recommendations come, respectively, from John E. B. Myers, "Abuse and Neglect of the Unborn: Can the State Intervene?" *Duquesne Law Review* 23:1 (1984), pp. 26–31; and Margery Shaw, "Conditional Prospective Rights of the Fetus," *Journal of Legal Medicine* 5:1 (1984), pp. 96–100.

52. Robertson, "Procreative Liberty," p. 445.

53. Phillip E. Johnson, "The ACLU Philosophy and the Right to Abuse the Unborn," *Criminal Justice Ethics* 9:1 (1990), p. 49.

54. Alan Dershowitz, "Drawing the Line on Prenatal Rights," *Los Angeles Times,* May 14, 1989, p. V5.

55. Ibid. One is tempted to ask Mr. Dershowitz if men's right to abuse their bodies stops at the border of their testicles, given the undeniable evidence of reproductive damage from male alcohol abuse (and the consequent harm inflicted on children born prematurely, or with low birth weight or birth defects, as a result).

56. Parness, "Crimes against the Unborn," p. 171.

57. Ibid., p. 117; citations omitted, emphasis added.

58. Ibid., p. 117.

59. Paul A. Logli, "Drugs in the Womb: The Newest Battlefield in the War on Drugs," *Criminal Justice Ethics* 9:1 (1990), p. 26.

60. Donald C. Bross, "Court-Ordered Intervention on Behalf of Unborn Children," *Children's Legal Rights Journal* 7:2 (1986), pp. 11–14.

61. Ibid., p. 12.

62. Johnson, "The ACLU Philosophy," p. 50.

63. Ibid., p. 51.

64. Nancy K. Rhoden, "The Judge in the Delivery Room: The Emergence of Court-Ordered Cesareans," *California Law Review* 74 (1986), pp. 1951–2030; quotation from p. 1953.

2. Bodily Integrity and Forced Medical Treatment

1. This account is taken from *In re* A.C., D.C. App. No. 87-609 (April 26, 1990), reversed by Judge J. Terry, as reported by *The Daily Washington Law Reporter* 118:110, pp. 1249–56, and Terry Thornton and Lynn Paltrow, "The Rights of Pregnant Patients: Carder Case Brings Bold Policy Initiatives," *Health Span: The Report of Health Business and Law* 8:5 (1991), pp. 10–16.

2. *In re* A.C., 573 A.2d 1235 (D.C. App. 1990).

3. Ibid.

4. Stoners v. George Washington University Hospital et al., Civil Action No. 88-05433 (Sup. Ct. D.C. 1990).

5. For relevant legal cases see D. Ortiz, "Privacy, Autonomy, and Consent," *Harvard Journal of Law and Public Policy* 12:1 (1989), and J. Rubenfeld, "The Right of Privacy," *Harvard Law Review* 4:4 (1989), pp. 737–807.

6. George J. Annas, "Forced Cesareans: The Most Unkindest Cut of All," *The Hastings Center Report* (June 1982), p. 16.

7. Flanigan, "Mom Follows Belief, Gives Birth in Hiding," *Detroit Free Press,* June 28, 1982, p. 3A, cited in Janet Gallagher, "Prenatal Invasions and Interventions: What's Wrong with Fetal Rights," *Harvard Women's Law Journal* 10 (1987), p. 47.

8. W. A. Bowes and B. Selgestad, "Fetal versus Maternal Right: Medical and Legal Perspectives," *American Journal of Obstetrics and Gynecology* 58 (1981), pp. 209–214. Details of this case are also reported in Annas,

"Forced Cesareans," pp. 16–45, and in Donald C. Bross, "Court-Ordered Intervention on Behalf of Unborn Children," *Children's Legal Rights Journal* 7:2 (1986), pp. 11–15.

9. Veronica E. B. Kolder, Janet Gallagher, and Michael Parsons, "Court-Ordered Obstetrical Interventions," *New England Journal of Medicine* 316:19 (1987), p. 1193.

10. James Hoefler and Brian Kamoie, "The Right to Die: A Developmental Analysis of Case Law and a Comparative Analysis of Statutes in the American States," paper delivered at the annual meeting of the Northeastern Political Science Association, Philadelphia, 1991.

11. "A Fetal Feat That Is a First," *U.S. News and World Report,* June 11, 1990, p. 16.

12. Andrew Purvis, "Major Surgery before Birth," *Time,* June 11, 1990, p. 55.

13. Gina Kolata, *The Baby Doctors* (New York: Delacorte, 1990), p. 29.

14. Lawrence J. Nelson and Nancy Milliken, "Compelled Medical Treatment of Pregnant Women: Life, Liberty, and Law in Conflict," *Journal of the American Medical Association* 259 (February 19, 1988), pp. 1060–66.

15. As quoted by Ruth Hubbard, in "Personal Courage Is Not Enough: Some Hazards of Childbearing in the 1980s," in Rita Arditti, Renate Duelli Klein, and Shelley Minden, eds., *Test-Tube Women: What Future for Motherhood?* (Boston: Pandora Press, 1984), p. 349.

16. In her history of surgery, Ann Dally points out that women have been both the victims and the beneficiaries of experimental medicine. This dynamic is still clearly at work in the case of reproductive and fetal technologies. See Ann Dally, *Women Under the Knife* (New York: Routledge, 1991).

17. For a general survey of techniques for fetal medical treatment see A. Kurjak, ed., *The Fetus as a Patient* (Elsevier, 1985).

18. Kim M. Davidson, Douglas S. Richards, Desmond A. Schatz, and Delbert A. Fisher, "Successful in Utero Treatment of Fetal Goiter and Hypothyroidism," *New England Journal of Medicine* 324:8 (February 21, 1991), p. 545.

19. Gina Kolata documents the development of fetal medicine in interviews with pioneering physicians in *The Baby Doctors: Probing the Limits of Fetal Medicine* (New York: Delacorte, 1990).

20. M. T. Longaker et al., "Maternal Outcome after Open Fetal Surgery: A Review of the First Seventeen Human Cases," *Journal of the American Medical Association* 265:6 (1991), pp. 737–741; quotation from p. 740.

21. Ibid.

22. N. Scott Adzick, quoted in Sharon Begley, "The Tiniest Patients," *Newsweek,* June 11, 1991, p. 56.

23. The term "maternal environment" is widely used in the prenatal medical literature; the *Newsweek* article cited above refers to the uterus as the "operating womb"; recall that Longaker et al. referred to the woman's womb as the "best possible intensive care unit" for the fetus after surgery.

24. As Valerie Hartouni observes, motherhood in these cases is reduced to the purest form of self-subordination: "what could be a more complete, absolute or total expression of maternal commitment, self-sacrifice and dedication than 'giving life after death'?" "Containing Women: Reproductive Discourse in the 1980s," unpublished paper (1989), p. 6. The phrase "give birth after death" is taken from a *Newsweek* article on the Henderson case, where a woman who was legally brain dead from a brain tumor was kept on life support for 53 days, long enough to nurture the fetus she was carrying until it could be delivered by cesarian section at 32 weeks' gestation.

25. Longaker et al., "Maternal Outcome after Open Fetal Surgery," p. 741.

26. J. R. Lieberman, M. Mazor, W. Chaim, and A. Cohen, "The Fetal Right to Live," *Obstetrics and Gynecology* 53:4 (1979), pp. 515–517.

27. Ronna Jurow and Richard Paul, "Cesarian Delivery for Fetal Distress without Maternal Consent," *Obstetrics and Gynecology* 63:4 (1984), pp. 596–598; quotation from p. 597.

28. Lieberman et al., "Fetal Right to Live," p. 515, emphasis added.

29. Ibid., p. 516.

30. As reported in Annas, "Forced Cesareans," p. 16.

31. Ibid.

32. See Jefferson v. Griffin Spaulding County Hospital Authority Ga. 87, 274 S.E.2d (1981). Details of this case are also reported in B. K. Rothman, *Recreating Motherhood* (New York: Norton, 1989), p. 166. See also Martha Field, "Controlling the Woman to Protect the Fetus," *Law, Medicine, and Health Care* 17:2 (1989), pp. 114–129, esp. p. 116, and Gallagher, "Prenatal Invasions and Interventions," p. 33.

33. Veronica Kolder, *Women's Health Law: A Feminist Perspective* (August 1985) pp. 1–2, unpublished manuscript on file at the Harvard Women's Law Journal, as quoted by Gallagher, "Prenatal Invasions and Interventions," p. 9.

34. Kolder, Gallagher, and Parsons, "Court-Ordered Obstetrical Interventions," pp. 1192–96; 1193. Two months later, the woman's husband committed suicide.

35. Lieberman et al., "Fetal Right to Live," p. 516.

36. Kolder, Gallagher, and Parsons, "Court-Ordered Obstetrical Interventions," p. 1192.

37. Annas, "Forced Cesareans," p. 16.

38. Bowes and Selgestad, "Fetal versus Maternal Right," pp. 209–214.

39. Kolder, Gallagher, and Parsons, "Court-Ordered Obstetrical Interventions," p. 1193. Not all information was reported by those completing the survey.

40. Quoted in Ronni Sandroff, "Invasion of the Body Snatchers: Fetal Rights vs. Mother's Rights," *Vogue,* October 1988, p. 331.

41. Bross, "Court-Ordered Intervention," p. 11; emphasis added. Bross also discusses cases involving drug abuse.

42. Ibid., pp. 11–12.
43. Ibid., p. 15.
44. See Janet Gallagher, "Prenatal Invasions and Interventions: What's Wrong with Fetal Rights," *Harvard Women's Law Journal* 10 (1987), pp. 9–58, esp. p. 48, n. 203.
45. Kolder, Gallagher, and Parsons, "Court-Ordered Obstetrical Interventions," pp. 1192, 1193.
46. Judge Margaret Taylor, quoted in Sandroff, "Invasion of the Body Snatchers," pp. 330–331.
47. Kolder et al. report that a sixteen-year-old pregnant girl in Wisconsin was held in secure detention for the safety of her fetus because she "tended to be on the run" and to "lack motivation or ability to seek prenatal care." Kolder, Gallagher, and Parsons, "Court-Ordered Obstetrical Interventions," p. 1195.
48. Ibid., p. 1192. It would be interesting to see how these attitudes were related to gender. No information on this breakdown was reported.
49. Cited in Sandroff, "Invasion of the Body Snatchers," p. 330.
50. *In re* A.C. at 1237.
51. American College of Obstetricians and Gynecologists, "Patient Choice: Maternal-Fetal Conflict," Committee on Ethics, Opinion Number 55, October 1987.
52. Ibid., p. 2.
53. These cases are: Raleigh Fitkin–Paul Morgan Memorial Hospital v. Anderson 201 A2d 537 (NJ 1964), cert. denied, 377 US 984, and Jefferson v. Griffin Spalding County Hospital Authority 274 S.E.2d 457 (Ga. 1981).
54. See for instance "The Fruit of Angela Carder's Agony," *New York Times*, Dec. 8, 1990, p. A24; and "Court in Capital Bars Forced Surgery to Save Fetus," *New York Times*, April 27, 1990, p. A3.
55. As reported in Thornton and Paltrow, "The Rights of Pregnant Patients," pp. 10–16.
56. As quoted in Linda Greenhouse, "Hospital Sets Policy on Pregnant Patient's Rights," *New York Times*, Nov. 29, 1990, p. 14.
57. Ibid.
58. ACOG guidelines, p. 1; emphasis added.

3. From Protecting the Woman to Privileging the Fetus

1. Other women involved in the case included one whose husband had had a vasectomy and two others who were in their fifties but had not yet experienced menopause (and so still fell into the company's category of "fertile" women). International Union, UAW v. Johnson Controls, Inc. 111 S.Ct. 1196 (1991), at 7. Details of the case can also be found in Eileen McNamara, "Factory and Fertility," *Boston Globe*, October 17, 1989, p. 1; "Risk to Fetus Ruled as Barring Women from Jobs," *New York Times*, October 3, 1989, p. A16; and "The Next Right to Life Battleground," *Christian Science Monitor*, December 13, 1989, p. 18.

2. UAW v. Johnson Controls, p. 7.

3. Catherine MacKinnon, *Toward a Feminist Theory of the State* (Cambridge, Mass.: Harvard University Press, 1989), p. 222.

4. These practices were documented in a study of fetal protection policies in the chemical and electronics industries in Massachusetts. See C. Daniels, M. Paul, and R. Rosofsky, "Family, Work, and Health Survey," Massachusetts Department of Public Health and University of Massachusetts Medical Center, 1985. Copies of this report are available from: Occupational Health Coordinator, Women's Health Division, Department of Public Health, 150 Tremont Street, Boston, MA 02111. See also M. Paul, C. Daniels, and R. Rosofsky, "Corporate Responses to Reproductive Risks," *American Journal of Industrial Medicine* 16 (1989), pp. 267–280.

5. An excellent example of normative policy analysis may be found in Lance deHaven-Smith, *Philosophical Critiques of Policy Analysis: Lindbloom, Habermas, and the Great Society* (Gainesville: University of Florida Press, 1988). For a discussion of theoretical constructs for policy analysis see M. E. Hawkesworth, *Theoretical Issues in Policy Analysis* (Albany: State University of New York Press, 1988). For an interesting analysis of how private concerns become public problems see Joseph R. Gusfield, *The Culture of Public Problems: Drinking-Driving and the Symbolic Order* (Chicago: University of Chicago Press, 1981), as well as Celeste Condit, *Decoding Abortion Rhetoric* (Urbana: University of Illinois Press, 1990).

6. Muller v. Oregon, 208 U.S. 412 (1908).

7. New York State, *Second Report of the Factory Investigating Commission* (1911), vol. 4, p. 2095.

8. Alice Kessler-Harris, *Out to Work* (New York: Oxford University Press, 1982), p. 188. Kessler-Harris provides a most interesting and provocative analysis of the internal debates over protective labor legislation at the turn of the century. Other works that address the history of protective labor law include Judith A. Baer, *The Chains of Protection: The Judicial Response to Women's Labor Legislation* (Westport, Conn.: Greenwood Press, 1978); Diane Balsar, *Sisterhood and Solidarity: Feminism and Labor in Modern Times* (Boston: South End Press, 1987); Deborah Rhode, *Justice and Gender* (Cambridge, Mass.: Harvard University Press, 1989); and Nancy Cott, *The Grounding of Modern Feminism* (New Haven: Yale University Press, 1987).

9. For a more complete analysis of legislation in New York see Chapter 3, "No Place for Women: Protective Labor Legislation for Women, New York, 1900–1925," in Cynthia Daniels, "Working Mothers and the State," Ph.D. diss., University of Massachusetts, Amherst, 1984. For an excellent historical analysis see Susan Lehrer, *Origins of Protective Labor Legislation for Women* (Albany: State University of New York Press, 1987).

10. For analysis of the exemption of homeworkers from protective labor legislation see Cynthia Daniels, "Between Home and Factory: Homeworkers and the State," in E. Boris and C. Daniels, eds., *Homework: His-*

torical and Contemporary Perspectives on Paid Work at Home (Urbana: University of Illinois Press, 1989).

11. See Kessler-Harris, Out to Work, on this point.

12. Wendy Williams, "Firing the Woman to Protect the Fetus: The Reconciliation of Fetal Protection with Employment Opportunity Goals under Title VII," Georgetown Law Journal 69 (1981), pp. 641–704; 647.

13. Johnson Controls Company document E-3/90, personal files of the author.

14. For companies identified here see Ronald Bayer, "Reproductive Hazards in the Workplace: Bearing the Burden of Fetal Risk," Milbank Memorial Fund Quarterly Health and Safety 60 (Fall 1982), pp. 633–656, esp. p. 635; Williams, "Firing the Woman," p. 647, n. 27.

15. In 1987, Digital Equipment Corporation instituted such a policy when a study commissioned by the company showed that women working in the microchip production rooms ("clean rooms") experienced miscarriage at twice the normal rate. Even though the study's methodology was seriously questioned by the scientific community, pregnant women were immediately banned from all areas of work deemed "hazardous" by the company and free monthly pregnancy tests were offered to women on site. As soon as a woman was identified as pregnant by the company physician, she was pulled from her work in the clean room and transferred into a non-production service job. Across the country, microchip producers followed Digital's lead, banning pregnant women from clean-room work and limiting the work of "fertile" women or women of childbearing age. For discussion of the Digital case and analysis of the weaknesses of its study see Daniels, Paul, and Rosofsky, "Family, Work, and Health Survey."

16. See Williams, "Firing the Woman"; Lisa J. Raines and Stephen P. Push, "Protecting Pregnant Workers," Harvard Business Review (May-June 1986), pp. 26–30.

17. UAW v. Johnson Controls 886 F.2d 871 (7th Circuit, 1989); hereafter cited as "UAW v. Johnson Controls (7th Circuit, 1989)." In addition to Johnson Controls, other companies have required women to prove their infertility, such as Eli Lilly, B. F. Goodrich, Goodrich Chemical, and the Bunker Hill Company of Idaho; see Jane Terry, "Conflict of Interest: Protection of Women from Reproductive Hazards in the Workplace," Industrial and Labor Relations Forum 15 (1981), pp. 43–55, esp. p. 50. For an analysis of the decision upholding Johnson Controls' policy in the Seventh Circuit Court of Appeals, see Suzanne Mager, "Courting Disaster: Judges, Workers, and the Case of Johnson Controls," New Solutions (Summer 1990), pp. 6–8.

18. Bayer, "Reproductive Hazards in the Workplace," p. 636.

19. Johnson Controls company document, E-3/90, personal files.

20. Michael J. Rosenberg, Paul J. Feldblum, and Elizabeth G. Marshall, "Occupational Influences on Reproduction: A Review of Recent Literature," Journal of Occupational Medicine 29 (1987), pp. 584–591.

21. Respondent's brief (for Johnson Controls) in UAW v. Johnson Controls, No. 89-1215 (1990), p. 1. The company presumes in this case that concerns for equality and concerns for fetal health are mutually exclusive.
22. Ibid.
23. Ibid.
24. Ibid., pp. 1–2, quoting Dr. Ellen Silbergeld in DEP JA 240.
25. Ibid., p. 3, citing UAW petition, quoting Chisholm.
26. Ibid., p. 2.
27. Ibid., p. 3, n. 4.
28. Ibid., p. 5.
29. Ibid., p. 6, n. 7. Since lead exposures may vary significantly from one work station to another in a given workplace, the most accurate measure of individual exposure is a blood test for lead. Safety standards may also set more general limits on the amount of lead in the air at a workplace.
30. Ibid., p. 7.
31. Ibid., p. 7, n. 6.
32. Ibid., p. 6.
33. Ibid., p. 7.
34. Ibid.
35. Ibid., p. 5.
36. Brief Amicus Curiae of the National Safe Workplace Institute, submitted in UAW v. Johnson Controls, No. 89-1215 (1990), p. 4.
37. Ibid., p. 18.
38. Ibid., p. 20.
39. Ibid.
40. UAW v. Johnson Controls (7th Circuit, 1989), p. 50, quoting from Torres v. Wisconsin Department of Health and Social Services 859 F.2d. at 1528.
41. Quoted in Terry, "Conflict of Interest," p. 48.
42. Ibid., p. 50.
43. Johnson Controls company document, E-3/90, personal files of the author.
44. Quoted in Bayer, "Reproductive Hazards in the Workplace," p. 644.
45. Quoted in Lynn Mattson, "The Pregnancy Amendment: Fetal Rights and the Workplace," Case and Comment 86 (1981), pp. 33–41; p. 33.
46. "Might not the State have an overriding interest in protecting future generations by allowing employers the right to exclude females from a workplace?" Ibid., p. 40.
47. Emily Martin makes a similar point about the disruptive nature of women's bodies in the capitalist industrial workplace in The Woman in the Body (Boston: Beacon Press, 1987), esp. chaps. 6 and 7.
48. See N. J. Gordon, "The Fetus as Business Customer in the Toxic Workplace: Wright v. Olin Corporation Sets Standards for Fetal Protection Programs," Detroit College of Law Review 4 (1984), pp. 973–996.
49. Johnson Controls company document, E-3/90, personal files of the author.

50. UAW v. Johnson Controls, No. 89-1215, Official Transcript Proceedings before the Supreme Court of the United States, Alderson Reporting Company, 1111 14th St. N.W., Washington, D.C., Oct. 10, 1990, hereafter cited as "Supreme Court transcript," pp. 24–25.

51. Supreme Court transcript, p. 25.

52. Supreme Court transcript, p. 28; emphasis added.

53. United States v. Vuitch 402 U.S. 62, 80 (1971), as quoted in Mattson, "The Pregnancy Amendment," p. 41.

54. Brief Amicus Curiae of Concerned Women for America, submitted in UAW v. Johnson Controls, No. 89-1215 (1990), p. 14.

55. Ibid., p. 10.

56. Ibid., p. 15.

57. Ibid., p. 24, quoting from Smith v. Brennan, 31 N.J. 353, 364, 157 A.2d. 497, 503 (1960).

58. Brief Amicus Curiae of the U.S. Chamber of Commerce, submitted in UAW v. Johnson Controls, No. 89-1215 (1990), p. 4.

59. Ibid. The EPA accomplishes this ban by refusing to grant certification to pesticide applicators who are pregnant.

60. These results are cited and detailed in the U.S. Chamber of Commerce brief.

61. U.S. Chamber of Commerce brief, p. 6.

62. Respondent's brief, p. 18. For legal reasons, Johnson Controls was required to argue that this particular form of gender discrimination was necessary to the "normal operation" of its business.

63. Brief Amicus Curiae of the U.S. Catholic Conference, submitted in UAW v. Johnson Controls, No. 89-1215 (1990), p. 10.

64. Ibid., p. 11.

65. NSWI brief, p. 15.

66. Ibid., p. 5.

67. Ibid.

68. U.S. Chamber of Commerce brief, p. 2.

69. Supreme Court transcript, p. 37.

70. Raines and Push, "Protecting Pregnant Workers," p. 26.

71. Supreme Court transcript, p. 39.

72. NSWI brief, p. 19.

73. Petitioner's brief (for the United Auto Workers) in UAW v. Johnson Controls, No. 89-1215 (1990), hereafter cited as "Petitioner's brief," p. 5, n. 5.

74. Brief Amicus Curiae in support of petition for a Writ of Certiorari to the U.S. Court of Appeals for the Seventh Circuit by American Civil Liberties Union, et al., submitted in UAW v. Johnson Controls, Supreme Court No. 89-1215 (1989).

75. Petitioner's brief, p. 5.

76. Rosenberg et al., pp. 584–591. For further information on male reproductive hazards see W. E. Daniell and T. L. Vaughan, "Paternal Employment in Solvent Related Occupations and Adverse Pregnancy Out-

comes," *British Journal of Industrial Medicine* 45 (1988), pp. 193–197; A. D. McDonald et al., "Father's Occupation and Pregnancy Outcome," *British Journal of Industrial Medicine* 46 (1988), pp. 329–333; D. A. Savitz, E. A. Whelan, and R. C. Kleckner, "Effect of Parents' Occupational Exposures on Risk of Stillbirth, Preterm Delivery, and Small-For-Gestational-Age Infants," *American Journal of Epidemiology* 129:6 (1989), pp. 1201–18.

77. Brief Amicus Curiae of Trial Lawyers for Public Justice, submitted in UAW v. Johnson Controls, No. 89-1215 (1990), p. 10.

78. Ibid., p. 4.

79. Brief Amicus Curiae of the American Public Health Association, submitted in UAW v. Johnson Controls, No. 89-1215 (1990), p. 53.

80. Ibid., pp. 53–54.

81. Ibid., pp. 54, 55, n. 60.

82. Joan Bertin, "Reproduction, Women, and the Workplace: Legal Issues," *Occupational Medicine: State of the Art Reviews* 1:3 (1986), p. 503.

83. UAW v. Johnson Controls (7th Circuit, 1989), p. 33.

84. There is some evidence that teratogens can be delivered to the fetus by a male in cases where the pregnant woman has sex with a man whose sperm (or spermatic fluid) is contaminated by a toxic substance.

85. Brief Amicus Curiae of the National Resources Defense Council, submitted in UAW v. Johnson Controls, No. 89-1215 (1990), p. 10.

86. Ibid., p. 11.

87. Ibid.

88. APHA brief, p. 49, n. 51.

89. NRDC brief, p. 11.

90. Ibid., p. 16.

91. Ibid., pp. 12–13.

92. Trial Lawyers brief, p. 23.

93. Brief Amicus Curiae of Equal Rights Advocates, et al., submitted in UAW v. Johnson Controls, No. 89-1215 (1990), p. 24.

94. Bertin, "Reproduction, Women, and the Workplace," p. 500; Terry, "Conflict of Interest," p. 45.

95. Donna M. Randall, "Women in Toxic Work Environments: A Case Study and Examination of Policy Impact," *Women and Work* 1 (1985), pp. 259–281; 259.

96. Terry, "Conflict of Interest," p. 49; Bertin, "Reproduction, Women, and the Workplace," p. 503.

97. Randall, "Women in Toxic Work Environments," p. 263.

98. Ibid., p. 269.

99. Quoted in the APHA brief, pp. 36 and 37.

100. Johnson Controls Company memorandum, "Fetal Protection Policy," May 1, 1989, approved by Jean M. Beaudoin.

101. Johnson Controls Company document, "GBD [General Battery Division] Position on Employee Sterilization," no date.

102. Johnson Controls Company internal memorandum, August 16, 1982, "Fetal Protection Policy," from E. A. Ross to GBD Plant Managers and

Plant Personnel Managers, Bulletin No. 3-954-01, Deposition Exhibit 8 (in 7th Circuit Case).

103. Ibid.

104. Ibid.

105. Petitioner's brief, p. 37.

106. Brief Amicus Curiae of the NAACP Legal Defense and Educational Fund, Inc., et al., submitted in UAW v. Johnson Controls, No. 89-1215 (1990), p. 49.

107. Ibid., p. 31.

108. Julie Barreto, "Women Farmworkers in California," *Golden Gate University Law Review* 10 (Summer 1980), pp. 1117–46, p. 1133.

109. Randall, "Women in Toxic Work Environments," p. 268.

110. Terry, "Conflict of Interest," p. 46.

111. Reply Brief for Petitioners, submitted in UAW v. Johnson Controls, No. 89-1215 (1990), p. 5.

112. Trial Lawyers brief, p. 13.

113. Ibid., p. 14.

114. Ibid., p. 5.

115. Brief Amicus Curiae of the Association of the Bar of the City of New York, et al., submitted in UAW v. Johnson Controls, No. 89-1215 (1990), p. 11.

116. Ibid., pp. 15–16.

117. Los Angeles Department of Water and Power v. Manhart 435 U.S. 707 (1978), as cited in New York Bar Association Brief, p. 11.

118. Ibid., p. 10.

119. Brief Amicus Curiae of the American Civil Liberties Union, et al., submitted in UAW v. Johnson Controls, No. 89-1215 (1990), pp. A-37–38.

120. Ibid., p. A-67.

121. Ibid., p. A-71.

122. Ibid., p. A-51–52.

123. Ibid., p. A-45–46.

124. Supreme Court transcript, pp. 35–36. Since identification of individual justices in oral hearing transcripts is prohibited by the Court, my personal notes were used for identification of justices quoted here.

125. Quoted in Carin Ann Clauss, Marsha Berzon, and Joan Bertin, "Litigating Reproductive and Developmental Health in the Aftermath of UAW v. Johnson Controls," paper delivered at Occupational and Environmental Reproductive Hazards conference, Woods Hole, Mass., 1991, p. 23.

126. For a more detailed discussion of the response of the EEOC and OSHA to this policy problem see Cynthia R. Daniels, "Competing Gender Paradigms: Gender Difference, Fetal Rights, and the Case of Johnson Controls," *Policy Studies Review* 10:4 (1991), pp. 51–68.

4. The Politics of Vengeance

1. Jennifer Clarise Johnson v. State of Florida, 77,831, Supreme Court of Florida, decision issued July 23, 1992. Quote from p. 17. Additional facts

of this case are taken from Johnson v. State 578 So.2d. 419, 420 (Fla. 5th DCA, 1991), and Amicus Brief of the American Public Health Association et al., Johnson v. State of Florida (Fla. 5th DCA, 1991).

2. Joseph Gusfield discusses the communicative function in his analysis of state regulation of drinking and driving, *The Culture of Public Problems: Drinking-Driving and the Symbolic Order* (Chicago: University of Chicago Press, 1981). A wide range of social theorists have pointed to the educative or expressive power of state authority, including Antonio Gramsci, Hannah Arendt, Max Weber, and John Kenneth Galbraith. For a discussion of the expressive power of public policy in the contemporary American context see Philip Heymann, "How Government Expresses Public Ideas," in Robert B. Reich, ed., *The Power of Public Ideas* (Cambridge, Mass.: Harvard University Press, 1988).

3. As Robert Reich observes, state actors give voice to "half-articulated fears and hopes . . . embodying them in convincing stories about their sources and the choices they represent." *The Power of Public Ideas,* p. 5.

4. Gusfield, *The Culture of Public Problems,* p. 148.

5. Judith Hicks Stiehm, "Women, Men and Military Service: Is Protection Necessarily a Racket?" in Ellen Boneparth, ed., *Women, Power and Policy* (New York: Pergamon Press, 1982), p. 292.

6. Liberal political philosophy (and law) operates on the premise that all social actions can be reduced to individual actions. The legal system is predicated upon the belief that causality can be located with the agency of individuals. This is problematic when analyzing social phenomena (like infant mortality) associated with social forces, where blame cannot be pinned on individuals.

7. See Gusfield, *The Culture of Public Problems,* esp. chap. 6.

8. James Bopp, the general counsel of the National Right-to-Life Committee, argues that prosecution encourages drug-dependent women to seek abortions and is thus ineffective in protecting fetal health. See Susan Diesenhouse, "Punishing Pregnant Addicts: Debate, Dismay, No Solutions," *New York Times,* Sept. 10, 1989, p. E5. All other associations listed have issued formal policy statements opposing prosecution.

9. See, for example, Katha Pollit, "A New Assault on Feminism," *The Nation,* March 26, 1990, pp. 409–418; Dawn Johnsen, "From Driving to Drugs: Governmental Regulation of Pregnant Women's Lives after Webster," *University of Pennsylvania Law Review* 138 (1989), pp. 179–215; Martha Field, "Controlling the Woman to Protect the Fetus," *Law, Medicine and Health Care* 17:2 (1989), pp. 114–129; and Dorothy E. Roberts, "Punishing Drug Addicts Who Have Babies: Women of Color, Equality, and the Right to Privacy," *Harvard Law Review* 104:7 (1991), pp. 1419–82.

10. Sergeant Van Hemert, quoted in Jan Hoffman, "Pregnant, Addicted— and Guilty?" *New York Times Magazine,* Aug. 19, 1990, p. 34.

11. Lynn M. Paltrow, "Criminal Prosecutions against Pregnant Women: National Update and Overview," Reproductive Freedom Project, American Civil Liberties Union Foundation, April 1992; and Lynn Paltrow and Suzanne Shende, "State by State Case Summary of Criminal Prose-

cutions against Pregnant Women and Appendix of Public Health and Public Interest Groups Opposed to These Prosecutions," American Civil Liberties Union memorandum, March 29, 1991. Prosecutions have been documented in Alaska, Arizona, California, Connecticut, District of Columbia, Florida, Georgia, Idaho, Illinois, Indiana, Kentucky, Massachusetts, Michigan, Mississippi, Missouri, Nevada, New York, New Hampshire, North Carolina, North Dakota, Ohio, South Carolina, South Dakota, Texas, Virginia, Washington, and Wyoming.

12. These statistics are compiled from Paltrow and Shende, "State by State Case Summary."

13. Jean Davidson, "Drug Babies Push Issue of Fetal Rights," *Los Angeles Times*, April 25, 1989, p. 1.

14. Testimony of attorney Kary Moss, of the American Civil Liberties Union, before the House Select Committee on Children, Youth and Families, "Law and Policy Affecting Addicted Women and Their Children," May 17, 1990, p. 213. Moss stated that "hundreds of children" had been removed from their mothers at birth in Illinois as a result of a single positive drug test.

15. See David Greenblatt, "Urine Drug Testing: What Does It Test?" *New England Law Review* 23 (1989), pp. 651-666, and J. Morgan, "Problems of Mass Urine Screening for Misused Drugs," *Journal of Psychoactive Drugs* 16:4 (1984), pp. 305-318.

16. State of Wyoming v. Pfannenstiel, 1-90-8CR, County Court of Laramie, Wyoming, complaint filed Jan. 5, 1990. The court later found no probable cause for her prosecution.

17. State of Missouri v. Lisa Pindar, 1991.

18. Melanie Green was the first woman charged with manslaughter on the grounds that her child's death was linked to her cocaine use during pregnancy. The charges were later dropped after a grand jury refused to indict her. People of the State of Illinois v. Green, 88-CM-8256, Cir. Ct., filed May 8, 1989.

19. State of Alaska v. Grubbs, 4FA S89 415 Criminal, Sup. Ct., Aug. 25, 1989.

20. State of Mississippi v. Oneaver McGrover Hart.

21. Commonwealth of Massachusetts v. Levey, 89-2725-2729 Superior Ct. of Mass., Dec. 4, 1989. The homicide case was dropped after the state failed to prove that the fetus died as a direct result of the auto accident (rather than from medical mistreatment). Levey was convicted of driving while intoxicated and sentenced to drug treatment. See Paul Langner, "Charge Dropped in Death of Fetus," *Boston Globe*, Dec. 5, 1989, p. 29.

22. State of North Carolina v. Inzar, 90 CRS 6960–61 Sup. Ct. of Robeson County, filed April 16, 1990, cited in Paltrow and Shende, "State by State Case Summary," p. 14.

23. Quoted in Paltrow and Shende, "State by State Case Summary," p. 3.

24. Paltrow, "Criminal Prosecutions," p. 24.

25. Paltrow and Shende, "State by State Case Summary," pp. 11–12.

26. Paltrow, "Criminal Prosecutions," p. 3.

27. Information on legislation is from Kary Moss, Gene Guerrero, and Kitty Kolbert, "Legislative Update on Drug Use During Pregnancy," American Civil Liberties Union memorandum, Sept., 16, 1991.

28. Ohio Senate Bill 82, still pending. Upon the woman's second conviction she would be required to "participate in a five-year program of monitored contraceptive use approved by the court." Quoted in Moss et al., "Legislative Update," p. 6.

29. North Carolina DRH 8082-LF (3.21), status pending; Rhode Island HBN 5104 (child abuse) and HBN 5108 (manslaughter), status pending in 1991.

30. Oregon SBN 347, status pending in 1991.

31. Idaho Senate Bill 1168.

32. Florida HB 1453; Montana SBN 190, effective January 1, 1992.

33. A *Family Circle* telephone survey of 768 randomly selected people found that 66 percent of those surveyed believed that a woman convicted of child abuse should have the birth control device Norplant surgically implanted as part of her criminal sentence. Edward Tivnan, "Life and Death Decisions: Should Child Abusers Be Sterilized? The New Moral Dilemmas," *Family Circle Magazine,* March 10, 1992, p. 99.

34. See Rorie Sherman, "Bioethics Debate," *The National Law Journal* 13:36 (1991), p. 1.

35. For a more detailed discussion, see Deanna S. Gomby and Patricia H. Shiono, "Estimating the Number of Substance-Exposed Infants," *The Future of Children* 1:1 (1991), pp. 17–25.

36. Marvin Dicker and Eldin A. Leighton, "Trends in Diagnosed Drug Problems among Newborns: United States, 1979–1987," paper presented at the annual meeting of the American Public Health Association, 1990. The study adjusted for underreporting by multiplying the actual number of reported cases by three. For a copy of this paper, write to Marvin Dicker, Financing and Services Research Branch, Division of Applied Research, NIDA, 5600 Fisher's Lane, Room 10-05, Rockville, MD 20857.

37. State of Florida v. Johnson, E89-890-CFA Fla. Cir. Ct., July 13, 1989. For details of this case, see also Kary Moss, "Substance Abuse during Pregnancy," *Harvard Women's Law Journal* 13 (1990), pp. 278–299.

38. For instance, see Linda Mayes, Richard Granger, Marc Bornstein, and Barry Zuckerman, "The Problem of Prenatal Cocaine Exposure," *Journal of the American Medical Association* 267:3 (1992), pp. 406–408.

39. Gomby and Shiono, "Estimating the Number of Substance-Exposed Infants," p. 23.

40. Ibid.

41. See Gladys Friedler, "Developmental Toxicology: Male-Mediated Effects," in Maureen Paul, ed., *Occupational and Environmental Reproductive Hazards* (Baltimore: Williams and Wilkins, 1993). Also see Ricardo A. Yazigi, Randall Odem, and Kenneth Polakoski, "Demonstration of Specific

Binding of Cocaine to Human Spermatozoa," *Journal of the American Medical Association* 266:14 (1991), pp. 1956–59.

42. Mary Harris, an analyst for the Orange County Social Services Agency, quoted in Davidson, "Drug Babies Push Issue of Fetal Rights."

43. Ira Chasnoff, "Drug Use and Women: Establishing a Standard of Care," *Annals of the New York Academy of Science* 562 (1989), pp. 208–210.

44. Davidson, "Drug Babies Push Issue of Fetal Rights."

45. Catherine Foster, "Fetal Endangerment Cases Increase," *The Christian Science Monitor,* Oct. 10, 1989, p. 8.

46. "Jail for 'Crack Moms'?" *The Christian Science Monitor,* Oct. 25, 1989, p. 20.

47. Jean Davidson, "Newborn Drug Exposure Conviction a 'Drastic' First," *Los Angeles Times,* July 31, 1989, p. 1.

48. Charlotte Low Allen, "Torts Are Taking Over for Morality," *Wall Street Journal,* June 9, 1989, p. A10.

49. Andrea Stone, "It's 'Tip of Iceberg' in Protecting Infants," *USA Today,* Aug. 25, 1989, p. 3.

50. Jane E. Brody, "Widespread Abuse of Drugs by Pregnant Women Is Found," *New York Times,* Aug. 30, 1988, p. 1.

51. Jane E. Brody, "Cocaine: Litany of Fetal Risks Grows," *New York Times,* Sept. 6, 1988, p. C1.

52. Herald Wire Service, "Cocaine Babies' Mom Convicted in Drug Trial," *Miami Herald,* July 14, 1989, p. 1.

53. "Cocaine: Litany of Fetal Risks Grows," p. C1.

54. Suzanne Delcamp, "Born Addicted," *Asbury Park Press,* Aug. 18, 1991, p. C1.

55. Ibid.

56. For findings of the most recent studies, see Ira Chasnoff et al., "Temporal Patterns of Cocaine Use in Pregnancy: Perinatal Outcome," *Journal of the American Medical Association* 261:12 (1989), pp. 1741–44; Barry Zuckerman et al., "Effects of Maternal Marijuana and Cocaine Use on Fetal Growth," *New England Journal of Medicine* 320:12 (1989), pp. 762–768; Linda C. Mayes et al., "The Problem of Cocaine Exposure: A Rush to Judgement," *Journal of the American Medical Association* 267:3 (1992), pp. 406–408; and H. Westley Clark and Meryle Weinstein, "Chemical Dependency," in Paul, *Occupational and Environmental Reproductive Hazards.*

57. This list is from "Born Addicted," p. C1.

58. Dr. Mehnur Abedin, quoted in Cathy Trost, "Born to Lose," *Wall Street Journal,* July 18, 1989, p. A1.

59. Joan Beck, "Women Are Killing or Stunting Their Babies with Cocaine," *Chicago Tribune,* Oct. 26, 1989, Section 1.

60. Tony Tague, Muskegon County Prosecutor, "Protection of Pregnant Addicts and Drug Affected Infants in Muskegon County, Michigan," Muskegon County Prosecutor's Office, Muskegon, Michigan, 1991, p. 3.

61. Wendy Chavkin, "Mandatory Treatment for Drug Use During Pregnancy," *Journal of the American Medical Association* 266 (1991), p. 1556.

62. "Drug Babies Push Issue of Fetal Rights."

63. Ibid.

64. For an analysis of the history and cultural construction of the "monster mother" see Anna Lowenhaupt Tsing, "Monster Stories: Women Charged with Perinatal Endangerment," in Faye Ginsburg and Anna Lowenhaupt Tsing, eds., *Uncertain Terms: Negotiating Gender in American Culture* (Boston: Beacon Press, 1990).

65. Michael Dorris, *The Broken Cord* (New York: Harper and Row, 1989), p. 146.

66. Alan Dershowitz, "Drawing the Line on Prenatal Rights," *Los Angeles Times,* May 14, 1989, p. V5.

67. Judge Frederick J. Kapala, quoted in "Cocaine Use in Pregnancy Amounts to Child Abuse, a Judge Rules," *New York Times,* May 4, 1989, p. A22.

68. Tague, "Protection of Pregnant Addicts," p. 5.

69. See Jeffrey Parness, "Crimes against the Unborn: Protecting and Respecting the Potentiality of Human Life," *Harvard Journal on Legislation* 22:97 (1985), p. 117.

70. Trost, "Born to Lose," p. A1. The woman who brought crack cocaine to the hospital reportedly died in the delivery room after she gave birth to the baby. Trost's article also reports that one 28-year-old woman addicted to crack showed up at the hospital with a dead newborn, and that other women have abandoned their children at birth; she also reports the case of a drug-dependent woman giving birth to her seventh child (presumably drug-affected).

71. Dorris, *The Broken Cord,* p. 165.

72. Ibid.

73. Christina Robb, "The Mind of a Scholar, the Heart of a Father," review of *The Broken Cord* in the *Boston Globe,* July 28, 1989, p. 38.

74. Ibid.

75. Patricia Guthrie, "Alcohol's Child: A Father Tells His Tale," review of *The Broken Cord* in the *New York Times Book Review,* July 30, 1989, p. 1 (emphasis added).

76. Phyllis Theroux, "The Tragic Inheritance," review of *The Broken Cord* in the *Washington Post,* July 1989.

77. Dorris, *The Broken Cord,* p. xvii.

78. Ibid., p. 79.

79. Ibid., p. 186.

80. Ibid., p. 166.

81. Carl A. Hammerschlag, "Substance Abuse as Child Abuse," review of *The Broken Cord* in the *Los Angeles Times,* July 30, 1989, p. 1.

82. Sue Trupin, a staff nurse at San Francisco General Hospital, quoted in Trost, "Born to Lose," p. A1.

83. Trost, "Born to Lose."

84. Compare Trost, "Born to Lose," with Tony Tague, "Protection of Pregnant Addicts," especially pp. 1–3.

85. Tague, "Protection of Pregnant Addicts," p. 2.

86. Dicker and Leighton, "Trends in Diagnosed Drug Problems among Newborns," p. 26.

87. Gomby and Shiono, "Estimating the Number of Substance-Exposed Infants," pp. 17–25.

88. Dicker and Leighton, "Trends in Diagnosed Drug Problems among Newborns," p. 14.

89. One could argue that the epidemic of "crack babies" corresponded quite closely with the two terms of the Reagan administration and the defunding of social welfare programs targeted to low-income communities.

90. Nesrin Bingol et al., "The Influence of Socioeconomic Factors on the Occurrence of Fetal Alcohol Syndrome," *Advances in Alcohol and Substance Abuse* 6:4 (1987), pp. 105–118.

91. Ibid., p. 117.

92. Ibid., pp. 110–111. The rates for these disorders are: hyperactivity, 12.2 percent vs. 39.6 percent; attention deficit disorder, 21.1 percent vs. 71.8 percent; congenital malformations, 9.2 percent vs. 45.9 percent. All of these were statistically highly significant or significant.

93. Jeanne Mager Stellman and Joan E. Bertin, "Science's Anti-Female Bias," *New York Times*, June 4, 1990, p. A23.

94. Gideon Koren et al., "Bias against the Null Hypothesis: The Reproductive Hazards of Cocaine," *Lancet* 2:8677 (1989), pp. 1440–42. See also G. Koren and N. Klein, "Bias against Negative Studies in Newspaper Reports of Medical Research," *Journal of the American Medical Association* 266:13 (1991), pp. 1824–26.

95. Daniel Coleman, "Lasting Costs for Child Found from a Mother's Early Drinks," *New York Times*, Feb. 16, 1989, p. B16.

96. Ibid.

97. Dorris, *The Broken Cord*, p. 199.

98. Quoted in Robb London, "Two Waiters Lose Jobs for Liquor Warning to Woman," *New York Times*, March 30, 1991, p. 7.

99. Cited in Karol L. Kumpfer, "Treatment Programs for Drug-Abusing Women," *The Future of Children* 1:1 (1991), p. 53.

100. Johnson v. State of Florida, Petitioners' Initial Brief, Appeal from the District Court of Appeal, Fifth District 77,831 Sup. Ct. of Fla. (1990), p. 31.

101. See Moss, "Substance Abuse during Pregnancy," p. 297. For further information on this suit contact Joan Bertin, Women's Rights Program, ACLU, 132 W. 43rd Street, New York, NY 10036. Administrators of programs which exclude pregnant women claim they don't have the resources to provide the special treatment pregnant women require, and they fear that the drugs used to treat addiction might harm fetal health. See Michael Freitag, "Hospital Defends Limiting of Drug Program," *New York Times*, Dec. 12, 1989, p. B9. One possible solution is to exempt treatment programs from liability in cases involving the treatment of

pregnant addicts, although such exemptions would undermine the programs' incentive to find appropriate and safe forms of drug treatment during pregnancy. The fear of liability may be unfounded, as none of these programs has ever been successfully sued on this basis.

102. I. J. Chasnoff, H. J. Landress, and M. E. Barrett, "The Prevalence of Illicit Drug or Alcohol Use during Pregnancy and Discrepancies in Mandatory Reporting in Pinellas County, Florida," *New England Journal of Medicine* 322 (1990), pp. 1202–1206.

103. Despite the scientific evidence, no one has yet suggested that public notices be posted warning men of the risks of testicular atrophy from the consumption of excessive amounts of alcohol. For a comprehensive survey of male reproductive effects see Gladys Friedler, "Developmental Toxicology: Male-Mediated Effects," in Paul, *Occupational and Environmental Reproductive Hazards*. Also see Ricardo A. Yazigi, Randall Odem, and Kenneth Polakoski, "Demonstration of Specific Binding of Cocaine to Human Spermatozoa," *Journal of the American Medical Association* 266:14 (1991), pp. 1956–59.

104. Frank Zuckerman et al., "Effects of Maternal Marijuana and Cocaine Use on Fetal Growth," *New England Journal of Medicine* 320 (1989), pp. 762–768.

105. B. Zuckerman, "Marijuana and Cigarette Smoking during Pregnancy: Neonatal Effects," in I. J. Chasnoff, ed., *Drugs, Alcohol, Pregnancy and Parenting* (London: Kluwer Publishers, 1988).

106. B. Zuckerman, "Drug-Exposed Infants: Understanding the Medical Risk," *The Future of Children* 1:1 (1991), pp. 26–35, and B. Zuckerman et al., "Maternal Psychoactive Substance Use and Its Effect on the Neonate," in A. Milunsky, E. A. Friedman, and L. Gluck, eds., *Advances in Perinatal Medicine* (New York: Plenum Press, 1986).

107. See Hortensia Amaro et al., "Violence during Pregnancy and Substance Use," *American Journal of Public Health* 80:5 (1990), p. 575.

108. On battering in general see Lenore Walker, *The Battered Woman Syndrome* (New York: Springer, 1984).

109. Michael Abramovitz, "Infant Mortality Soars Here," *Washington Post*, Sept. 30, 1989, p. A1.

110. Howard French, "For Pregnant Addicts, a Clinic of Hope," *New York Times*, Sept. 29, 1989, p. B1.

111. Beth Glover Reed, "Developing Women-Sensitive Drug Dependence Treatment Services: Why So Difficult?" *Journal of Psychoactive Drugs* 19:2 (1987), pp. 151–164.

112. Ibid., p. 155.

113. See American Public Health Association amicus brief in Johnson v. State of Florida (1991), p. 7.

114. On the idea of principled intervention and bases for judgments about parental competency see Bonnie Robin-Vergeer, "The Problem of the Drug-Exposed Newborn: A Return to Principled Intervention," *Stanford Law Review* 42 (1990), pp. 780–795.

115. "In the current context of the scarcity and poor quality of drug treatment programs for women/mothers, a debate over mandatory treatment is symbolic at best and is meaningless in practical terms." Wendy Chavkin, "Mandatory Treatment for Drug Use during Pregnancy," *Journal of the American Medical Association* 266 (1991), p. 1556.

116. Charles Taylor, "Foucault on Freedom and Truth," in David Couzens Hoy, ed., *Foucault: A Critical Reader* (New York and Oxford: Basil Blackwell, 1986), p. 71.

117. The paradox of revenge is very well captured by Terry Aladjem in his piece on capital punishment: "Now the mysterious process of the execution aspires to teach an abstract lesson about justice to an audience of would-be offenders, and it seems that finally a message in pain has been elegantly converted into a lesson about the terms of reciprocity and respect. [The painful punishment] serves as a warning that would instill public fear in order to insure a climate of respect, but by its very nature such a threat undermines the voluntarism of respect and reciprocity that we have identified with democracy." Terry Aladjem, "Revenge and Consent . . . ," unpublished paper, Social Studies Department, Harvard University (1991).

5. Toward a New Body Politics

1. See Anita Allen, *Uneasy Access* (Savage, Md.: Rowman and Littlefield, 1988), for a thorough exploration of the concept of privacy for women.

2. Wendy Brown makes a similar point in "Reproductive Freedom and the Right to Privacy: A Paradox for Feminists," in Irene Diamond, ed., *Families, Politics and Public Policy* (New York: Longman, 1983). Also see her longer treatment of this issue in *Manhood and Politics* (Savage, Md.: Rowman and Littlefield, 1988. On the Marxist idea of the "political swindle" of the liberal democratic state see Fred Block, *Revising State Theory* (Philadelphia: Temple University Press, 1987), and Martin Carnoy, *The State and Political Theory* (Princeton, N.J.: Princeton University Press, 1984).

3. The cases brought by Tony Tague as Muskegon County Prosecutor are documented in "Protection of Pregnant Addicts and Drug-Affected Infants in Muskegon County, Michigan" (Muskegon County Prosecutor's Office, 1991).

4. Eileen McDonagh makes the interesting argument that fetal personhood does not necessarily undermine women's right to self-sovereignty and bodily integrity. It only implies that women should have the right to consent to the use of their bodies for the benefit of another being. See Eileen McDonagh, "From 'Pro-Choice' to 'Pro-Consent' in the Abortion Debate: Guaranteeing Pregnant Women's Corporeal Sovereignty," unpublished paper, 1992, available from Murray Research Center, Radcliffe College, Cambridge, MA 02138.

5. On this point, see Z. Eisenstein, *The Female Body and the Law* (Berkeley: University of California Press, 1989).

6. On this point see Wendy Brown, *Manhood and Politics*. A number of theorists have recently addressed the question of citizenship for women, including Mary Dietz, "Context Is All: Feminism and Theories of Citizenship," in Jill Conway, Susan Bourque, and Joan Scott, eds., *Learning about Women, Gender Politics, and Power* (Ann Arbor: University of Michigan Press, 1987), and Kathleen B. Jones, "Citizenship in a Woman-Friendly Polity," *Signs* 15:4 (1990), pp. 781–812. On the relationship between gender and militarism see Jean Elshtain and Sheila Tobias, eds., *Women, Militarism, and War* (Savage, Md.: Rowman and Littlefield, 1990).

7. Emily Martin makes a similar point regarding menstruation and work in *The Woman in the Body* (Boston: Beacon Press, 1987), esp. chap. 7, "Premenstrual Syndrome, Work Discipline, and Anger."

8. For a good example of this argument see Wendy Kaminer, *A Fearful Freedom: Women's Flight From Equality* (Reading, Mass.: Addison-Wesley, 1990).

9. Maureen Paul, *Reproductive Toxicology* (in press).

10. Sonya Michel and Seth Coven, "Womanly Duties: Maternalist Politics and the Origins of Welfare States in France, Germany, Great Britain, and the United States, 1880–1920," *American Historical Review* 95:4 (1990), p. 1076.

11. Michel and Coven also note, in "Womanly Duties," that maternalist political proposals (such as programs for maternal and child health care) have to wait for a national crisis "like war or class conflict" to create an opening for their initiatives. Maternalist arguments have been able to compel the state to act only when such proposals were linked to more conservative social concerns, like pronatalism (in the case of maternal and child health) or the control of the labor force (in the case of protective labor law).

12. Alice Kessler-Harris, *A Woman's Wage* (Lexington: University of Kentucky Press, 1990), p. 55. A wide range of social welfare initiatives were originally introduced under the guise of gender protectionism. The Mothers' Pension Program in the nineteenth century laid the groundwork for more general welfare reform in the twentieth century. Maternity leave policies in the twentieth century are now laying the groundwork for parental and family leave for all workers. See Theda Skocpol, *Protecting Soldiers and Mothers: The Political Origins of Social Policy in the United States* (Cambridge, Mass.: Harvard University Press, 1992).

13. Anna Tsing analyzes reports of women murdering or abandoning their children in "Monster Stories: Women Charged with Perinatal Endangerment," in Faye Ginsburg and Anna Lowenhaupt Tsing, eds., *Uncertain Terms* (Boston: Beacon Press, 1990).

Acknowledgments

BAD METAPHORS are an occupational hazard of writing about reproductive politics. Nevertheless it is true that, like pregnancy, book-writing is both an intensely private and an essentially social experience. I have many people to thank for their contributions to this book. This work represents an attempt to integrate practical politics with a theoretical inquiry into the nature of gender power relationships. It is the product of my association with a diverse range of people—from union activists, lawyers, and workers, to feminist theorists, political scientists, and legal scholars. In my work, I have tried to build bridges between the "applied" and "academic" communities.

This book would not have been written without the assistance of the Bunting Institute at Radcliffe College. At a time when I was about to abandon all hope of integrating my political work with academic research, the Bunting Institute gave me a place from which to start anew. I am indebted to Ann Bookman, for making public policy important at the Institute, and to Florence Ladd, for her grace and spirited support during my Bunting year. My sister-fellows from that year played an important role in setting me on the course of this book, and each deserves special thanks: Bina Agarwal, Prilla Bracket, Janeen Clookey, Nona Glazer, Mitzi Goheen, Erica Harth, Gail Hershatter, Gail Hornstein, Marie Howe, Zella Luria, Isabel Marcus, Sonya Michel, Susan Porter, Lynn Randolph, Sonya Rose, Janet Seiz, and Dessima Williams.

I have been privileged to work with some of the most astute policial strategists in the feminist and labor communities and I'm deeply indebted to them for their insights. For an education in practical politics, I would like to thank Lisa Dodson and Nancy

Lessin. I would also like to thank my friends at the Women's Health Division in the Massachusetts Department of Public Health: Maria Aguiar, Elba Crespo, Iris Garcia, Davy Um Heder, Corinne Lidsky, Milagros Padilla, Robert Rosofsky, Celia Savitz, Beverly Smith, and Candace Waldron. I would also like to thank Maureen Paul for her insights and support of my research. I am deeply indebted to the women of the Massachusetts Coalition for Occupational Safety and Health for their first-hand experience and wisdom. Thanks go, in particular, to the women on the health and safety "front lines": Tolle Graham, Suzanne Mager, Elise Morse, and Cathy Schwartz. In gratitude, portions of any proceeds generated by this book will be donated to the Women's Reproductive Hazards Coalition of MassCOSH.

The legal activists and scholars who handled the court cases analyzed here have provided me with invaluable help. In particular, I'd like to thank Joan Bertin, of Columbia University's Project on Gender, Science and Law, and Lynn Paltrow, of the Center for Reproductive Law and Policy, for their patience and expertise.

I would like to thank my colleagues at two universities for their support. For two years, I had the pleasure of teaching at Harvard University in Women's Studies and Social Studies. My colleagues there were gracious and my students energetic and challenging. In particular, I would like to thank Judy Vichniac, Barbara Johnson, Terry Aladjem, and Andrea Walsh for their support. My students and research assistants have my special thanks, especially Melissa Hart, Susan Stayn, Rachel Harris, and Rachael Green. My new colleagues at Rutgers University have shown me that there is, indeed, a home for women and politics in the discipline of political science. Sue Carroll, Linda Zerilli, and Dick Wilson deserve special credit for their generous and enthusiastic support of my work.

I have been extremely fortunate to have worked with Angela von der Lippe at Harvard University Press. I would also like to thank Jean Elshtain for her (as always) challenging and insightful comments on the manuscript, and Mary Katzenstein and Molly Shanley for their substantive comments on my work. I am grateful to Zillah Eisenstein at Ithaca College for making me a feminist and a theorist. Paula Rayman taught me what it meant to be a scholar-activist, and I am grateful to her for her support at a critical juncture in my life. My thanks as well to Eileen McDonagh, who, with her sharp wit and insight, has kept me on my intellectual toes over the course of this project.

The memory of one woman was with me throughout the writing of this book—Mae Papastamos, my daughter's first day-care provider. Mae, along with her daughter Helen, was brutally murdered by Helen's estranged husband in November 1989. The contrast between our society's obsession with questions of fetal health and its casual disregard of violence against women was shocking as I lived through the loss of Mae—a woman who had dedicated herself to the preservation of life and the care of young children. I hope this book in some way can honor her memory.

The solitary act of writing is made possible by the work and support of many other people. I have been blessed with a wonderful family and life-long friends who have helped me in countless ways throughout this process. My deepest love and appreciation go to my mother, Margaret Daniels, for cooking (and cooking and cooking) and for caring for my daughter with the same great love with which she has always cared for me. She has taught me what it *really* means to be smart. For asking me the tough questions and for many years of moral support, thanks go to my sisters, Andrea Scott, Peggy Daniels, and Barbara Klinger. For extraordinary child care, I'd like to thank Margaret Schofield. For Friday night pizza and beer, thanks to Libba, Peter, Greta, and Faye; for helping me navigate (and survive) Harvard University, thanks to Beata; for the great reunions, thanks to Monte, Martha, Louise, Paul, Randy, Mary, Bernie, and Chris.

Finally, this book is dedicated to the two people whose love and labor are mixed in some way with every word. For Bob Higgins, my life-partner, thanks for promising to do the things that most men never think of and for actually delivering. For almost two decades, Bob has helped me past all the hurdles. For Katherine Rae, my daughter, thanks for keeping my lap warm at the computer and for being an extraordinary child. Their love and affection have animated this work and have helped me keep the politics of fetal rights (and book-writing) in perspective.

Index